DCPL0000310021

KV-277-163

EXPLORING

IRELAND'S
HISTORIC TOWNS

E X P L O R I N G

IRELAND'S
HISTORIC TOWNS

PAT DARGAN

The
History
Press
Ireland

The assistance of the Dublin Institute of Technology
in this production is gratefully acknowledged.

By the author of:

Exploring Georgian Dublin
Exploring Irish Castles

First published 2010

The History Press Ireland
119 Lower Baggot Street
Dublin 2, Ireland
www.thehistorypress.ie

© Pat Dargan, 2010

The right of Pat Dargan to be identified as the Author
of this work has been asserted in accordance with the
Copyrights, Designs and Patents Act 1988.

All rights reserved. No part of this book may be reprinted
or reproduced or utilised in any form or by any electronic,
mechanical or other means, now known or hereafter invented,
including photocopying and recording, or in any information
storage or retrieval system, without the permission in writing
from the Publishers.
British Library Cataloguing in Publication Data.
A catalogue record for this book is available from the British Library.

ISBN 978 1 84588 976 0

Typesetting and origination by The History Press
Printed in Great Britain
Manufacturing managed by Jellyfish Print Solutions Ltd

CONTENTS

GLOSSARY OF TERMS

Artisan Housing: Nineteenth-century housing, built specifically to house crafts and trades people.

Axial: Street plan, aligned on an architectural feature.

Barbican: Outer tower of a town gate.

Bastion: Arrow-shaped tower, projecting outwards from main wall of defence.

Burgage: Town building plot in medieval times.

Burgess: Tennant who leased a burgage in medieval times.

Colonial: Period of the Norman conquest of Ireland, between 1169 and 1500.

Cross-Linear Street: Two streets intersecting at right angles to one another.

Charter: Royal authorisation to undertake an action.

Early Christian: Period in Irish history between the fifth and tenth centuries that equates with the emergence of Christianity.

Enclosure: Area of land enclosed by physical barrier such as a wall or palisade.

Estate: Area of land in single ownership.

Fabric: The architecture of a town.

Feudalism: Social order that operated in medieval Europe, where an individual owed service to an overlord.

Garden Square: Town square laid out in the form of garden.

Georgian: Period in history that equates approximately with the reigns of the Hanoverian kings in Britain. In Ireland from about 1700 to 1845.

Gridiron: Pattern of streets arranged at right angles to one another.

Linear Street: Street laid out in a straight line.

Longphort: Viking ship harbour.

Mall: Street laid out with an extended central landscape feature.

Market Square: Town square used for market.

Market Colonisation: The gradual infilling of a market area with permanent buildings.

Medieval: Historic period, in Ireland from about the tenth to the sixteenth century.

Motte-and-Bailey: A temporary castle, consisting of a pair of earthen mounds with wooden defences.

Moat: A defensive water-filed trench surrounding a structure or town.

Murage Grant: Medieval grant authorising a town to raise money for town defences through taxation.

Normans: Colonists of Norman origins who arrived in Ireland from England and Wales, in the late twelfth century.

Octagon: Open space arranged in the form of an octagon.

Pale: Area of English rule around Dublin, particularly during the late medieval period.

Plantation: Period in Irish history during the sixteenth and eighteenth centuries, when English and Scottish settlers were introduced.

Rendering: Protective skin applied to the outside of a building (often referred to in Ireland as external plaster).

Renaissance: Post–medieval historical phase, which saw a revival of Classical study and ideals across Europe.

Suburb: Development outside of main area of a town.

Town Promotion: Ecclesiastical and Viking settlements raised to town status during the Norman period.

Town Wall: Defensive wall built around a town.

Victorian: Period in history that equated approximately to reign of Queen Victoria, in Ireland from around 1845 to 1914.

Vikings: Scandinavian raiders and settlers.

Wattle: Lightweight walling made with woven sticks and faced with mud.

Wide Streets Commission: Town planning body that operated in Dublin during the eighteenth and nineteenth centuries.

ONE

THE HISTORIC IRISH TOWN

800 – 1900

IRISH CITIES AND TOWNS

In the European context, Irish town foundation had a late start. In fact, nearly a thousand years separates the establishment of the Roman towns in Britain and the first appearance of what can be regarded as settlement centres on the Irish landscape, which took place in about the ninth century. This initial movement was followed later by the building of a range of towns during the subsequent Viking, Norman, Plantation, Georgian and Victorian periods. The effect of this movement was to give Ireland a dynamic, but often underestimated, urban legacy. It is the hope of this guide to encourage the general reader to experience and enjoy this legacy.

The story of Irish town development, as far as this guide is concerned, begins with the Early Christian settlements of the ninth century and ends at the close of the Victorian period. Within this time scale, Irish towns developed in a series of historical phases over a long period of time, rather than from a master plan implemented in a single movement. The guide explores the historical context and characteristic features that mark each of these phases. The social and political contexts that lay behind each phase are highlighted, the individuals responsible for the town developments are identified, and the motivation and ideals that prompted the developments are explored.

Despite the fact that Irish towns emerged and developed in different historic periods, they still manage to share a range of common town planning components. These include: a formal town plan, streets, public spaces, street architecture, and town defences. Taken together, these components can be considered as the building blocks of Irish towns and cities. Therefore, before looking at the individual development phases of the Irish town development movement, it is worth pausing to look at these components in detail.

PLAN

The plan of most Irish towns is made up of a number of streets arranged in a grid or similar geometric pattern. The grid form was one of the most common planning devices used throughout Europe, as it was seen to reflect the essence of town planning – geometry, discipline and simplicity. On a practical level, it is simple to set out on the ground and easy to extend. In the case of a simple grid, the streets are laid out so as to cross one another, and can be regular or irregular, depending on the street pattern. The term 'gridiron' is used where the layout follows a rigid chequerboard pattern of streets and cross streets laid out at right angles to one another. For example, the Georgian sector of Limerick city was laid out on an almost perfect gridiron plan (Fig. 1), whereas the layout of Armagh city incorporates both a curved and a radiating street pattern (Fig. 2). The lands between the various streets are called 'blocks' and these make up the basic units of the town plan. These blocks are, in turn, sub-divided into the building plots, where the houses and buildings were erected. These are usually long and narrow, with the narrow ends fronting onto one of the streets. This allows for the fitting of as many plots as possible into a given street length.

STREETS

The streets of most Irish towns fall into three types: linear, axial, or cross-linear (Fig. 3). The linear street is by far the simplest and consists of a clear passage through which people or vehicles can pass and which is usually lined on both sides with buildings. Streets are usually laid in a straight line, but curved or angled streets are not uncommon. The axial street is similar in idea to the linear street, except that the street terminates at a specific feature such as a building or gateway at one end. For example, St Stephen's church in Dublin acts as a closing feature at the end of Upper Mount Street (Fig. 4).

Leabharlanna Poibli Chathair Bhaile Átha Cliath
Dublin City Public Libraries

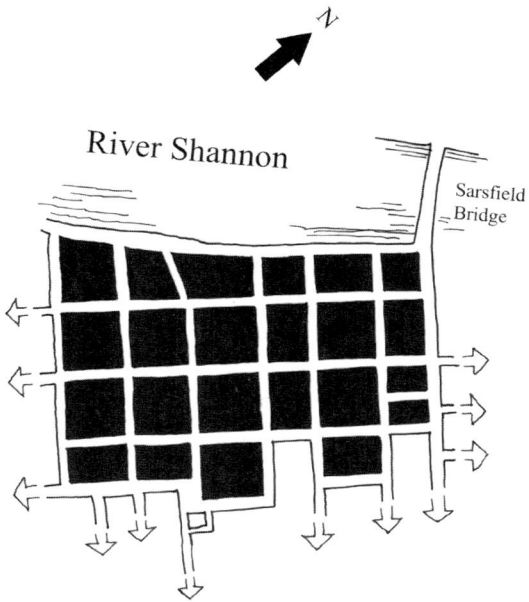

Fig. 1: Gridiron street plan, Georgian sector, Limerick, County Limerick.

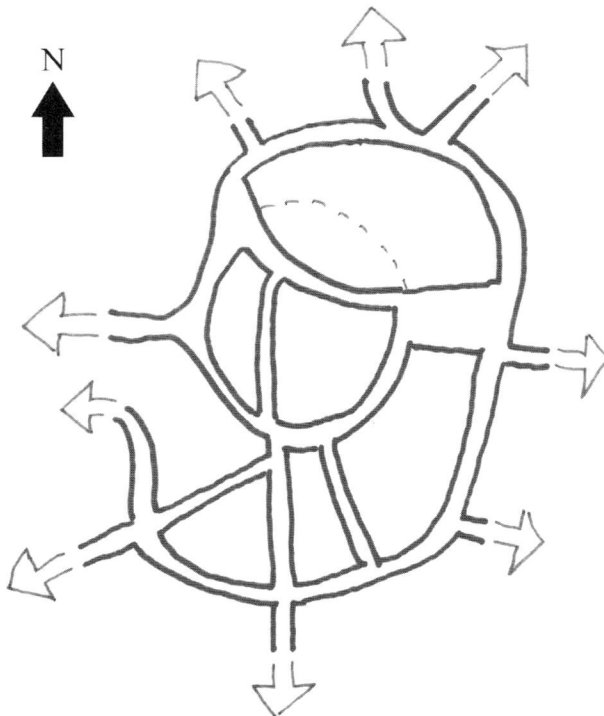

Fig. 2: Curved street plan with radiating roads, Armagh, County Armagh.

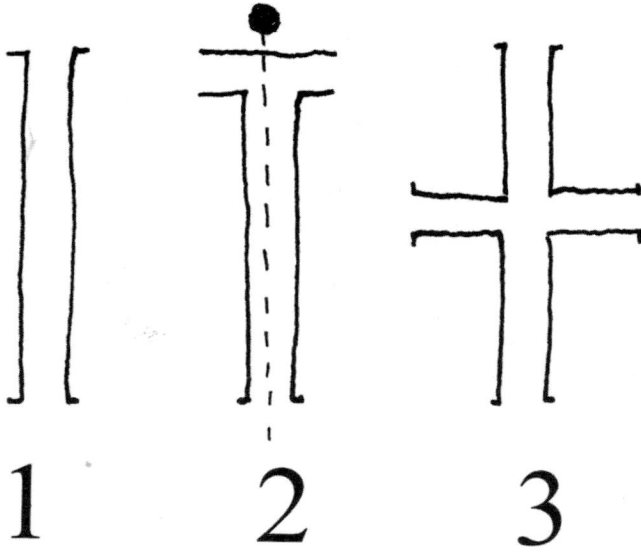

Left: Fig. 3: Street plan types: (1: Linear. 2: Axial. 3: Cross–Linear.)

Below: Fig. 4: Axial street, Upper Mount Street, Dublin.

PUBLIC SPACE

Most towns were given at least one public open space or square, often by leaving one of the town blocks free of building. In town planning, the term 'square' refers to the use rather than to the shape. For example, Mount Pleasant Square in Dublin has curved sides, while Fitzwilliam Square in Wicklow is triangular in layout. The market square, as its name suggests, took the form of a large open area, usually paved, where the town market was held. It could be square, rectangular, triangular, or wedge-shaped in plan. The garden square, on the other hand, tended to have a more environmental aspect. It was usually square or rectangular in plan and consisted of a central landscaped garden, enclosed by a railing and a roadway. In a number of instances, particularly during the Georgian and Victorian periods, towns were given both types of open spaces. Mitchelstown in County Cork, Warrenpoint in County Down (Fig.5), and Wicklow town (Figs 6 & 7), for example, were all given both a market and a garden square.

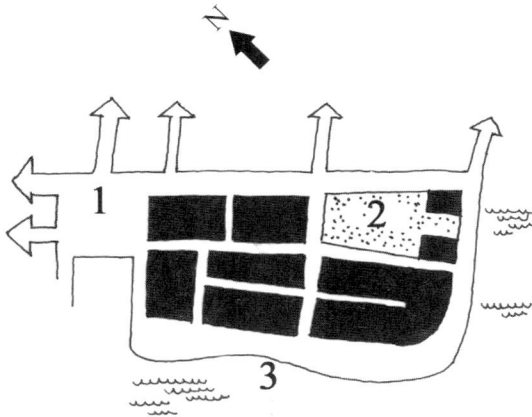

Left: Fig.5: Town plan, Warrenpoint, County Down (1: Market Square. 2: Garden Square. 3: Sea.)

Below: Fig.6: Open market square Wicklow, County Wicklow.

Fig.7: Fitzwilliam garden square, Wicklow, County Wicklow.

DEFENCES

During the medieval period, town defences were considered vital, and most Irish towns were given town walls, defended gateways, and a moat. During the following Renaissance period, however, such defences were considered unnecessary. The town walls were often neglected, or removed; town gates were demolished and new walls were no longer built. Despite this, a surprising number of Irish towns still retain stretches of their medieval walls, often hidden away. In the cases of Athenry in County Galway, Fethard in County Tipperary, and Derry City, considerable lengths of the town walling remain intact today, although these are not always accessible. In a most unusual example, the town moat in Loughrea in County Galway still operates as it did in the middle ages.

STREET ARCHITECTURE

The architecture, or fabric, of most Irish towns is uniformly Georgian or irregularly Victorian in character, such as can be found in Westport, County Mayo (Fig.8) or Warrenpoint, County Down (Fig.9). The reason for this is that, during the eighteenth and nineteenth centuries, the architecture of the earlier phases was swept away, during redevelopment works. This sometimes leads to the mistaken impression that all Irish towns date from the Georgian or the Victorian periods. Fortunately, the medieval fabric of a number of centres does survive and this can include castles, churches, monasteries, tower houses, and town defences. As a result, a significant number of Irish towns retain examples of their pre–Georgian fabric.

Ardee in County Louth, for instance, has a pair of fifteenth-century tower houses, as well as a medieval church and college, while Kells in County Meath has an Early Christian church and a round tower, as well as part of the medieval town wall. However, these pre-Georgian elements are not always obvious, although searching them out will prove rewarding. St Laurence Street in Drogheda, for example, offers a good example of this. In the thirteenth century, the street was laid out, leading to the town gate. Today, none of the original streetscape survives and the street is lined with Georgian and Victorian buildings – in many ways masking the street's medieval origins (Fig.10). The opposite is the case with the Georgian and Victorian towns, where the town plans, open spaces and street architecture survive intact to a very large degree indeed.

Fig.8: Uniform Georgian streetscape, Westport, County Mayo.

Fig.9: Irregular Victorian streetscape, Warrenpoint, County Down.

Fig. 10: St Laurence Street, Drogheda, County Louth.

TWO

EARLY CHRISTIAN SETTLEMENT

800 – 1200

URBAN ORIGINS

Irish town building began in around the eight century, when communities of monks and nuns established monasteries all around the country. These early monasteries consisted of oval-shaped sites surrounded by earth-built enclosures or wooden stockades. The purpose of the enclosure is uncertain, but it probably marked the boundary between the religious communities and the outside world. It also, of course, provided protection from wild animals or attackers. A particular feature of many of these early monasteries was the main approach route, which came from an eastern direction – although the purpose of this orientation is uncertain. Figure 11, presents a conjectural view of a typical Early Christian monastery site. The boundary is marked by a wooden stockade, around which runs a track or roadway and the eastern approach road is suggested. Inside the boundary is a church, some of the monks' huts, and a cross.

In a number of instances, particularly in the case of large sites, the area of the monastery was enlarged. This was achieved by building a second oval-shaped enclosure outside the original. However, this was not always the rule. Finglas, in County Dublin, was a large site with a single enclosure; Armagh and Glendalough were both given an inner and outer enclosure, while Nendrum, in County Down, had three enclosures, one outside the other. In the case of the double enclosure sites, such as Kells in County Meath, the inner enclosure acted as the religious core of the monastery. It contained a range of buildings including churches, cells, high-crosses, a cemetery, and occasionally a round tower. The outer enclosure, on the other hand, seems to have had a more secular function and often possessed craft and workshop facilities.

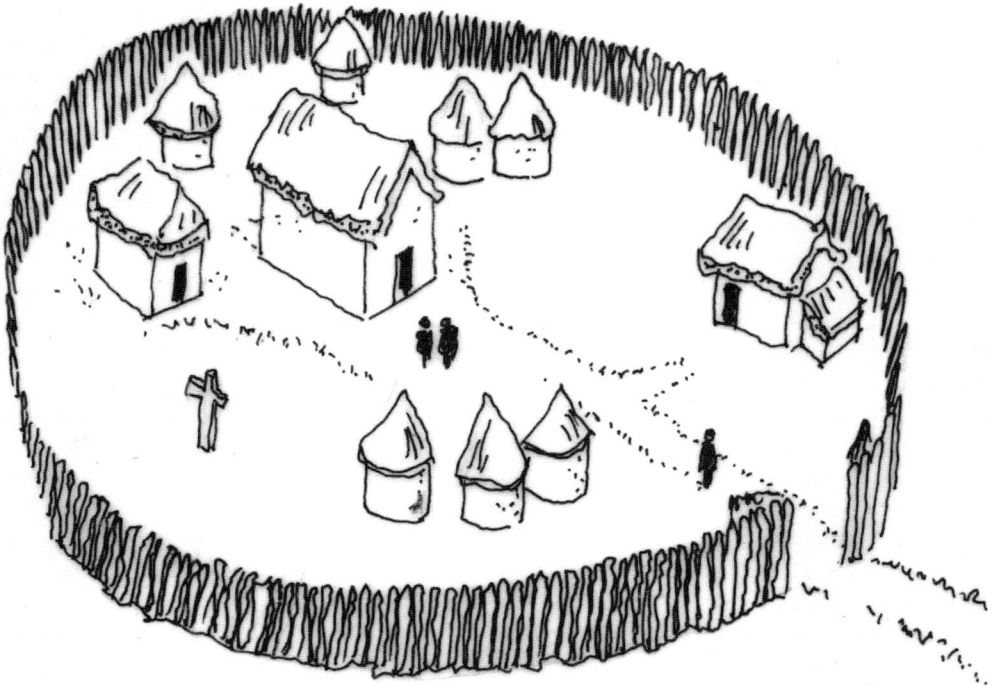

Fig.11: Conjectural view, Early Christian monastery site.

TOWN FOUNDATION

With the passage of time and through a process not yet understood, a number of these Early Christian monasteries developed into early towns. It is unclear whether these were towns in the true sense of the word, so they are usually referred to as settlements. For the most part, these settlements retained the oval shape of the original monastery, particularly in the case of the double enclosure examples. The inner core area retained its purely religious nature, while the outer enclosure became more secular in use. At the same time the curved boundary lines between the two enclosures evolved into a curved road system, with one roadway outside the other. The eastern approach route retained its importance and a triangular market area developed, at a point where the approach road met the curved road line. In addition, the settlement often became the hub of intersecting roads.

The period during which this transition from monastery to settlement took place is uncertain, but it can probably be dated to around the eight or ninth century. Also, the reason for the transition is uncertain. Clonmacnoise, Glendalough, and Monasterboice were all significant Early Christian monasteries that failed to develop into towns. On the other hand, a number of smaller sites such as Duleek in County Meath, Lusk in County Dublin and Tuam in County Galway emerged as successful towns, and even today they carry the imprint of their Early Christian origins in their circular street plans. It is indeed a remarkable fact that the ninth-century layout of these early settlements remains at the core of so many of Ireland's towns to this day.

SPACE AND FABRIC

Despite the uniformity of their overall form, not a great deal is known about the scale, street arrangements, or property divisions within these early settlements. There are historical references to paved streets, rows of houses and extensive populations, but little is known about how the initial sites were selected, how the internal roads were laid out, and how the building plots were apportioned. Equally, little is known about the architecture of the settlements, as little now remains except for the occasional round tower or the very rare stone-built religious building. The probability is that most of the buildings were wooden, none of which has survived. Notwithstanding this low level of survival, a significant number of Irish towns offer examples where the curved Early Christian circular street arrangement survives to this day and act as historic town centres. These include Armagh, Kells, and Kildare.

ARMAGH

The small city of Armagh, in County Armagh, represents the most notable example of the survival of an Early Christian layout into modern times. Here, the double circular street pattern, positioned on the crown of a steep hill, signals the centralised core of the city and testifies to its Early Christian origins. The original monastery is said to date from the fifth century foundation of St Patrick who, it is claimed, established his principal church here.

The characteristic oval inner enclosure of the monastery is traceable in the curved course of Castle Street and Callan Street (Fig. 2). This street line is incomplete in the northern sector; but the complete oval form can be traced in the property boundaries that still survive in this area. The outer enclosure circuit is equally clear and is highlighted by the curve of the outer circular road, which continues from the north of the complex right around to the west – with only a stretch in the north-western corner missing. The plan also highlights the sequence of roads that stretch outwards from the central core. Chief amongst these is the principal eastern approach road, that enters the market place and links the inner and outer roadways. The market place is now rectangular, but in its initial form, it may have been triangular. With the exception of the cemetery in the inner core, little of the ecclesiastical features of Armagh survive, although two churches, a library, high crosses, a priory, and a round tower are known to have existed within the complex.

KELLS

In a similar but less obvious fashion, the town of Kells in County Meath displays its Early Christian origins. This foundation was established in the early ninth century by a group of monks who had fled Iona, in the wake of Viking raids on the monastery there. From Figure 12, it can be seen that the street pattern possesses the characteristic double circular plan. At the centre of the existing town lie the remains of the inner core of the monastery. The inner roadway winds around this core on the north, east and on the south sides (Fig.12). Outside the inner enclosure, the course of the outer roadway — the line of Fair Green, Carrick Street (Fig.13), Castle Street, and Cross Street — follows the same circular pattern again on the north, east and, to a lesser extent, on the south side. Furthermore, the main approach route to the town — John Street — is from the east and is clearly identifiable, as is the triangular market area, which has been built over in the past.

Inside the inner core, ranges of early medieval buildings also testify to the early foundation date of the settlement. These include a round tower and a group of stone high crosses. A most unusual survival from the Early Christian period is the small stone-built church, St Columba's House, on the east side of Church Street (Fig.14).

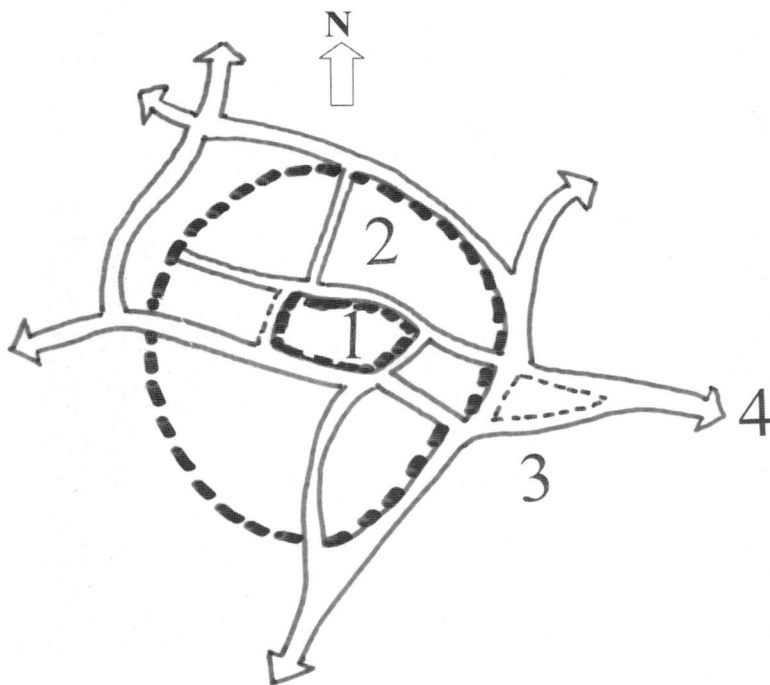

Fig.12: Plan of Kells, County Meath.
(1: Inner Enclosure.
2: Outer Enclosure.
3: Market Place.
4: Eastern Approach Road.)

Fig. 13: Carrick Street, Kells, County Meath.

Fig. 14: St Columba's House, Church Street, Kells, County Meath.

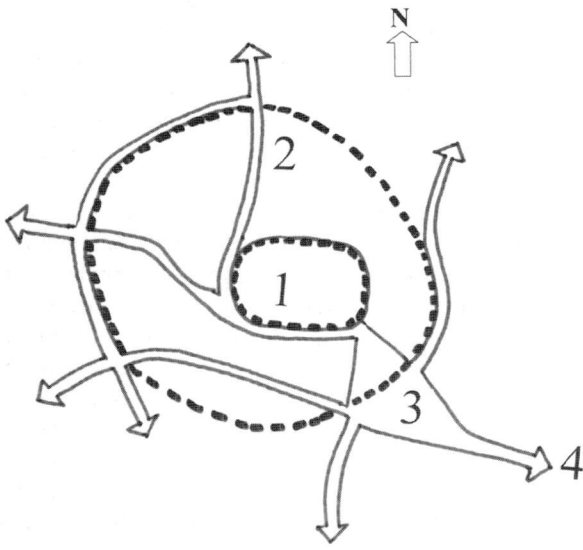

Fig. 15: Plan of Kildare, County Kildare. (1: Inner Enclosure. 2: Outer Enclosure. 3: Market Place. 4: Eastern Approach.)

Fig. 16: Triangular market place, Kildare, County Kildare.

KILDARE

The layout of the county town of Kildare express the principles of its Early Christian planning. This was a double monastery, for both monks and nuns, which has been dated to the sixth century and attributed to St Brigid. As is the case in Armagh and Kells, the curved pattern of the streets clearly reflects the double enclosure lines of the original settlement, although the line of the outer enclosure no longer exists along the northern and southern edges (Fig.15).

The line of the inner enclosure can, however, be identified by the boundary lines of the cathedral grounds. Church Lane marks south and west boundaries, while the site boundaries mark the remaining sides. Within the inner enclosure, a round tower and high crosses highlight the settlement's Early Christian origins. Well outside of this, the lines of White Abbey Street and Nugent Street on the west and east side, mark the outer limit of the complex. There is no road line to identify the southern boundary, but the curved property boundaries, at the back of the houses on the south side of Claregate Street, reflect the survival of this line. Similarly, the north-eastern boundary has also vanished, so that the line shown in Figure 15 must be seen as approximate. One of the most interesting elements of Kildare is the triangular market area that still partially fulfils its Early Christian purpose. The triangle is focused on the eastern approach road, Dublin Street, and is positioned between the inner and outer enclosure lines. Today the visitor to Kildare can still look across the triangular market area and see the round tower of the inner core (Fig.16).

The significance of the Early Christian settlements is that they made three important contributions to the national town building movement. First, they introduced the idea of urban settlement to the country. Secondly, these settlements went on to act as a base for subsequent town developments; Cork, Dublin, and Kilkenny are all examples that later evolved into important towns. Thirdly, the introduction of the curved street pattern and its eastern approach introduce town planning elements that, even today, act as the core for many Irish towns and villages. This was the state of the Irish town foundation and building when, during the ninth century, a new force arrived and imposed a fresh influence on Irish town development: the Vikings.

THREE

THE VIKING TOWNS

800 – 1200

THE VIKINGS

The second phase in the development of Irish towns was undertaken by the Vikings, during the ninth century. At this period Ireland, in common with most of Western Europe, was subjected to a series Viking raids. The first attack on the country took place in 798, when the monastery at Lambay Island, off the coast of Dublin, was sacked and destroyed. Thereafter, for the next hundred years or so, waves of similar attacks continued. Attracted by the wealth of the Irish monasteries, the Vikings arrived by sea, raided the monasteries and than disappeared back out to sea with their captured goods. Towards the middle of the ninth century, the frequency of the Viking raids increased and, in about 841, the first permanent bases were set up in Annagassen in County Louth and in Dublin. These were 'longphorts'. That is sheltered harbours that allowed the Vikings to over-winter in Ireland for the first time. Soon after, additional Viking posts were established around the Irish coast.

TOWN FOUNDATION

The infant settlements were usually sited within the shelter of river estuaries. These were close to the sea and at the same time they offered secure bases from where raids could be launched into the interior of the country. Apart from this, little is known about how the sites were selected by the Viking town founders. One curious feature that was common to all of the Viking settlements – with the exception of Waterford – was their location adjacent to the earlier Early Christian settlements, such as in Dublin, Cork and Wexford. It is uncertain whether or not Vikings took over the earlier settlements, or reached some sort of agreement where both existed side by side.

COASTAL NETWORK

A Viking settlement had been established in Limerick by the middle of the ninth century and this was followed slightly later by centres at Cork and Waterford, although the settlement at Annagassen did not survive. With the passage of time, the raiding stations became permanent and they evolved into a network of coastal towns. In this way, the towns of Arklow, Cork, Dublin, Limerick, Waterford, Wexford, and Wicklow all owe their origins and coastal locations to the Viking raiders (Fig.17). It is interesting to note that the names Arklow, Waterford, Wexford, and Wicklow are all of Viking origin.

The town layouts selected by the Vikings were based mainly on linear streets, the lines of which were governed by the site features rather than from any formal town plan. Recent archaeological excavation has revealed that these streets were lined with building plots on which were built rectangular wooden houses (Fig.18). Nothing, however, is known of how the plots were set out or how ownership was decided.

VIKING DUBLIN

The development of Viking Dublin was carried out in two stages. The first stage began in about 971, on the south bank of the River Liffey estuary. The site chosen consisted of a rectangular area of ground, formed by the double bend of the River Poddle where it entered the Liffey. The site had two important features. Firstly, a large pool had formed at the corner where the Poddle turned northwards before entering the Liffey. This was the Black Pool or 'Dubh Linn' in Gaelic, which ultimately gave the town its name. Secondly, a high ridge stretched across the site roughly parallel to the Liffey. In effect, the site offered the Vikings a naturally defended position

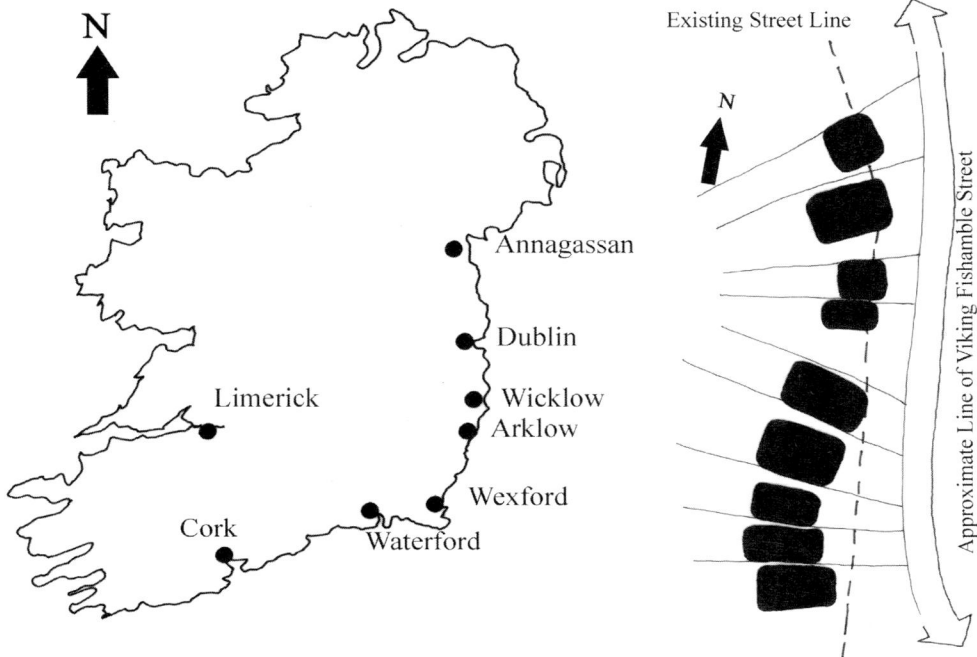

Above left: Fig. 17: The Viking town network.

Above right: Fig. 18: Conjectural plan, Viking Fishamble Street, Dublin, *c.* 1050.

that gave direct access to the Irish Sea. A natural moat was provided by the two rivers and the Black Pool offered a sheltered harbour for the Viking fleet. Coupled with these advantages, one could cross the Liffey a short distance upstream, at a point where a series of land routes joined before crossing the river.

Stage 1

In laying out their new town, the Vikings took advantage of the site's natural defences. The main street followed the line of the central ridge, the present line of Castle Street and Christchurch Place. This was intersected about half way along its length by two curved cross streets: Fishamble Street and Werburgh Street. The former curved northwards in a slope to the bank of the Liffey, while the latter led southwards, also in a slope, to the north bank of the Poddle. It is probable that the early town also had a system of lesser streets, although the precise details of these are uncertain. It is also possible that a fort was built in the south-eastern corner of the town, overlooking and protecting the ship harbour. Finally, the rectangular shaped settlement was enclosed by a defensive earthen bank (Fig. 19).

Stage 2

Where the line of Christchurch Street left the Viking town on the west side it divided into two routes. One – the current High Street – continued westwards running parallel to the Liffey, while the other – the current Nicholas Street – veered southwards. At this point the roads formed a Y-shaped pattern and this developed into a suburb, the second stage in the town's development. In the meantime, the Viking population had adopted Christianity and work began on the construction of Holy Trinity Church. The site chosen for the church lay at the junction of Christchurch Place and Fishamble Street, the present precinct of Christchurch Cathedral. This was the highest point in the town, and was followed later by the building of a number of further churches randomly located around the town. Later on, the suburb and the original settlement were merged when both were enclosed by a stone-built town wall, which gave the town its rectangular riverside form (Fig.20). Apart from the street pattern little survives of Viking Dublin.

VIKING WATERFORD

In the case of Waterford, the presence of Viking raiders was noted as early as about 853. This suggests a mid-ninth century date for the establishment of the Viking town, although the presence of a longphort was not recorded until 914. Here, as in Dublin, the position and form of the site played a major role in the site selection and in the laying out of a town plan. The shape of the site consisted of a triangular shaped area of land, near the mouth of Waterford Harbour, where the small St John's River flowed into the River Suir – much as was the case in Dublin. The triangular shape was bounded on the north by the main river and on the south by the tributary. It offered a natural fortified site that commanded the Suir and its estuary.

The initial Viking town plan seems to have consisted of a single street, Peter Street, that, like Dublin, was laid out along the line of a ridge which crossed the site from east to west. Here again, as was the case in Dublin, the town expanded westwards along this line in a series of stages (Fig.21). These expansion stages are probably reflected in the curved cross streets of the town, such as Henrietta Street and Exchange Street. In a similar way, the two secondary streets that run parallel to the Peter Street axis may also represent the early Viking street patterns. In any event, the result was the emergence of a triangular shaped Viking town, with a central axial street supported by a range of secondary streets.

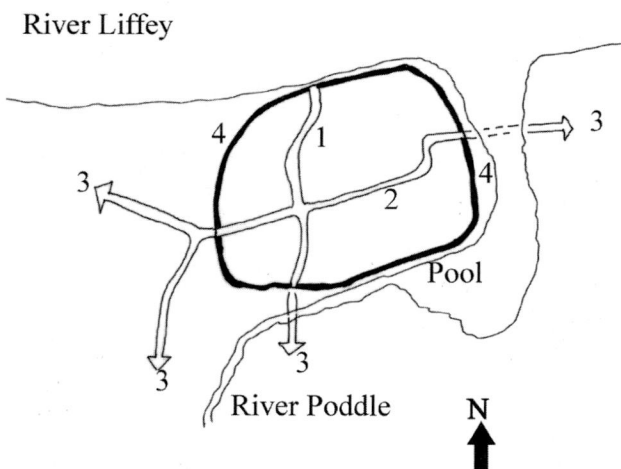

Fig.19: Viking Dublin, Phase 1, c.950.
(1: Fishamble Street. 2: Castle Street.
3: Route Way. 4 Town Wall)

River Liffey

4

1

3

5

2

3

4

Pool

3

3

River poodle

N

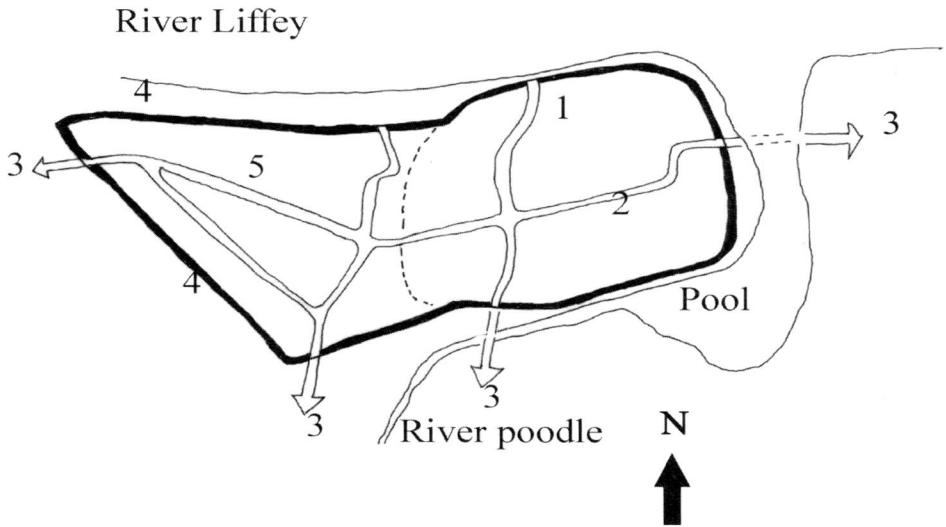

Fig.20: Viking Dublin, Phase 2, c.1100. (1: Fishamble Street. 2: Castle Street. 3: Route Way. 4 Town Wall. 5: High Street.)

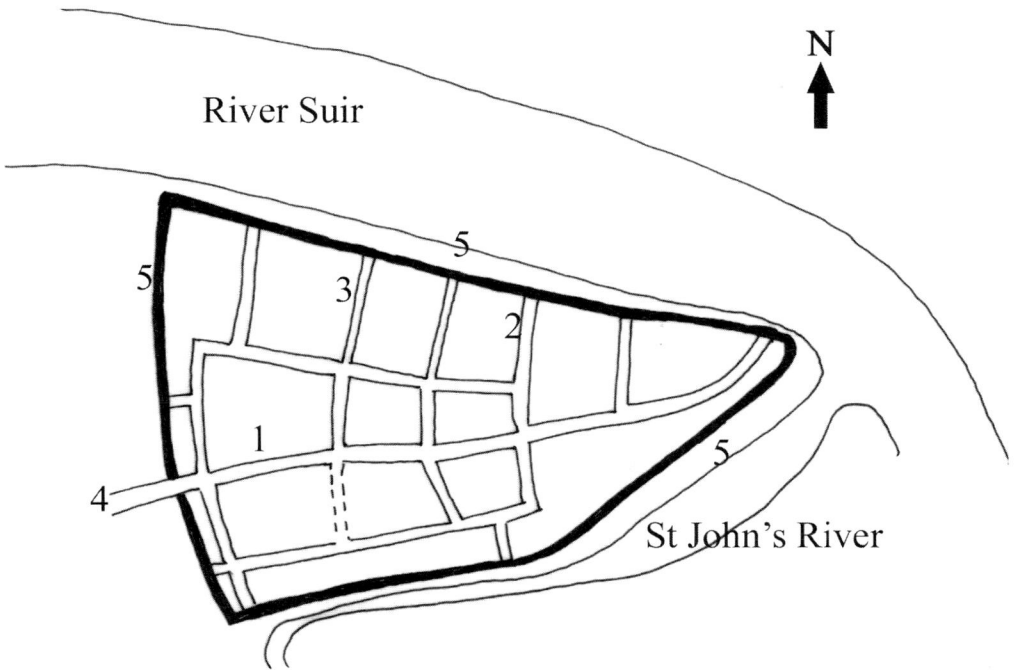

N

River Suir

5

5

3

2

1

5

4

5

St John's River

Fig.21: Viking Waterford, c. 1100. (1: Peter Street, 2: Henrietta Street, 3: Exchange Street. 4: Route Way. 5 Town Wall.)

Also, as in the case of Viking Dublin, Holy Trinity Cathedral was founded in the early years of the eleventh century and was located on the south side of the Peter Street. This was followed by a series of parish churches that were mainly distributed along the main axis. On the landward side of the new town, the western defences were built in the form of a continuous earthen bank which stretched from the River Suir southwards, as far as the St John's River, so as to join the two waterways together, in effect closing the base-line of the triangle and defending the new settlement. This bank was subsequently replaced by a stone wall that was eventually extended around the banks of the rivers to enclose and defend the town.

Very little is known about the location and form of the other Viking towns. However, taken as a whole, these Viking towns made three significant contributions to the development of the Irish town network. First, they laid into place the second phase of the national town network, by establishing a string of major ports around the Irish coast. Today, these ports still act as the principal components of that network, and give it its distinctive coastal emphasis. Even today, the country does not possess a single large inland city; secondly, the axial street patterns of Dublin and Waterford are still major streets in their respective cities; and thirdly, the Vikings were responsible for the introduction of what was to be a recurrent theme in the development of the Irish town system. As each further wave of colonists arrived in the country, it was closely followed by a period of town building. In effect, the town foundation process in Ireland became closely linked to colonisation — a feature which was to repeat itself again and again. Long after the Viking period, the Norman, Tudor, and Stuart colonists all left their marks on Ireland's town development.

As the close of the twelfth century approached, the Irish town network consisted of a range of coastal Viking towns and a number of inland Early Christian settlements. Then, in the late summer of 1169, the opening sequence of the Norman conquest of Ireland was launched, and a whole new range of town planning forces, concepts and ideals were introduced into the country.

FOUR

NORMAN TOWN
PLANNING

1170 − 1500

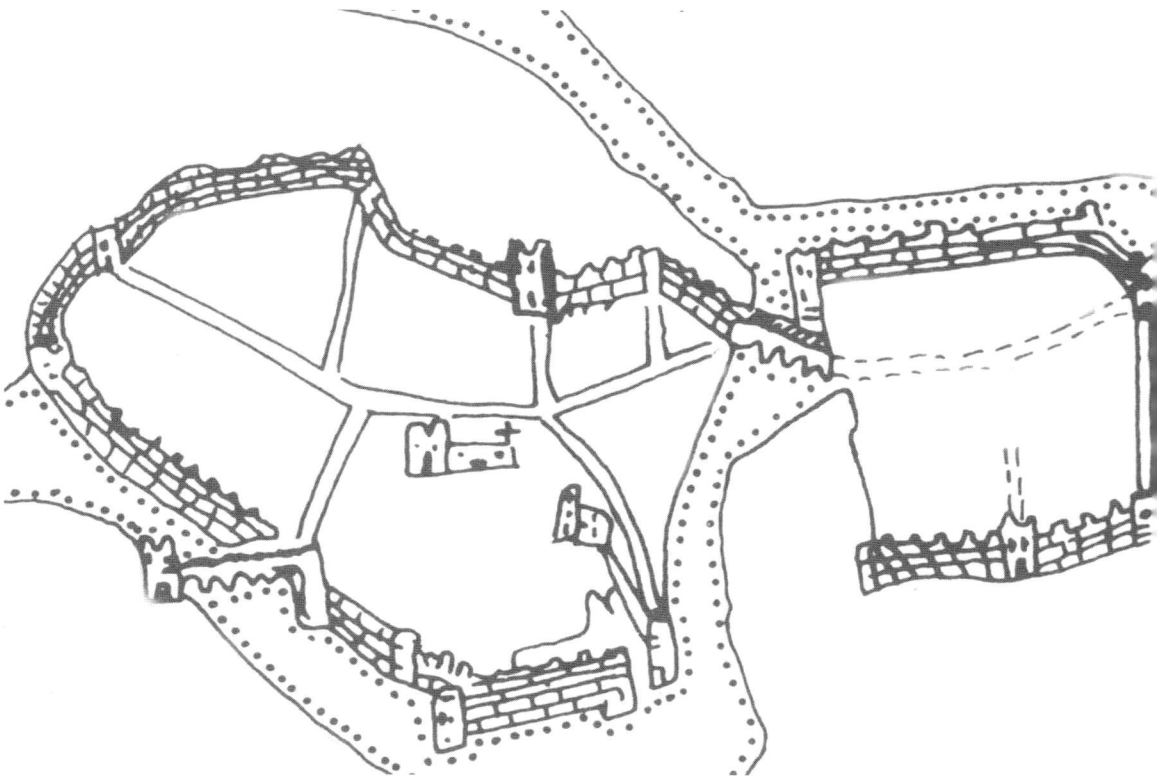

THE NORMANS

The third, and by far the most extensive, phase of the Irish town foundation process took place between the twelfth and fifteenth centuries, as part of the Norman conquest of the island. It is also the phase about which most information is available. During this phase, the Early Christian settlements and Viking towns were re-modelled and an extensive network of new towns was created across the Irish landscape. The arrival of the Normans in Ireland corresponded in time with the development of a major town-building movement in Europe, during which countries such as France, Germany, Poland, Spain, Switzerland, and Russia all experienced a wave of dramatic urban growth, where existing towns were enlarged and totally new towns were founded. With the Norman conquest of Britain, in 1066, the ideals of the new-town movement were introduced into England and later into Wales.

The Norman experience in Wales is of particular relevance to Ireland, as it was from southern Wales that the leaders of the early Normans came to Ireland. Here, in the hundred years prior to the conquest of Ireland, the ruling Norman families had acquired a high level of skill in town development. The motivation for town building was, above all else, a desire for profit. Profits in the form of rents derived from the leasing of the building plots. It is hardly surprising then, that when the Norman barons arrived in Ireland, they brought with them this motivation for profit and their town development skills. Once they took control of an area in Ireland, the operation of the town development was launched and was completed in eight systematic stages. These included the following:

1. The acquisition of land for town development.
2. The choosing of a suitable site.
3. The preparation of a town plan.
4. The introduction of settlers to live in the town.
5. The building of the town fabric.
6. The development of a town market.
7 The issuing of a town charter.
8. The creating of town defences.

LAND ACQUISITION

The first stage of the Norman town development, the acquisition of land, began in 1171 when Henry II granted the freshly-conquered territories in Leinster to his major barons, such as Richard de Clare and Hugh de Lacy. On receipt of the lands from the king, the barons divided their new territory into smaller land parcels, and then granted these parcels to the more minor barons, while retaining large areas of the King's grant for their personal use. Following this, the minor barons divided up their allocated lands and then granted them to lesser barons in the form of a manor: this being the basic land holding unit in Norman Ireland. Payment for most levels of land grants was initially in the form of military service, although this gradually gave way to cash payments over time. In effect, land-holding in the Irish colony was based on a system of feudal land grants and it was from all levels of this land grant system that the colonial town builders were drawn. Finally, it is worth noting, that the colonial town creation process was driven, above all else, by a desire for profit. Profit to the town developers and their descendants, in the form of rents derived from the leasing of the building plots.

CHOICE OF SITE

In total about sixty-six towns were founded by the Norman colonists across the country, although the greatest number of these lay in the eastern areas of the country (Fig.22). The

Normans never succeeded in taking the entire country, as the mountainous and western areas of the country remained in the hands of the Gaelic rulers. For this reason, the colonial town foundation operation was largely an eastern one, restricted to the areas of the country that lay under Norman control. Where Norman influence was at its strongest – in the eastern counties – the density of town foundation was at its maximum. In contrast, where colonial influence was weakest in western areas, town foundation was scarcer.

In colonial Ireland, as elsewhere in medieval Europe, town development fell into two main categories: existing settlements which were taken over and 'promoted' and new towns which were built or 'planted' on green field sites. In colonial Ireland, it was the Viking ports and Early Christian settlements that attracted the initial attention of the Normans. This can be seen from the speed with which the Viking coastal towns were secured. Wexford, Waterford and Dublin were taken within the first few months of the initial Norman invasion in 1169, although it was not until three years later the southern ports of Limerick and Cork were occupied and garrisoned.

It is not difficult to identify the reasons for the Norman interest in the Viking ports. By their very presence, they offered a network of ready-made bases which were distributed around the coast, particularly on the east and south. In a similar manner, the inland Early Christian settlements also acted as centres of potential development, and little time was lost in taking and promoting centres such as Kells in County Meath, as well as Kildare and Kilkenny in the counties of the same name.

Fig.22: Distribution of Norman towns in Ireland.

Where the Viking towns and the Early Christian settlements were concerned, the Normans had little choice in terms of selecting a site. They had to make do with the sites as they found them. Such restrictions did not, of course, apply in the case of a new planted town, and here the choice of a suitable location could be made, although even here, there were limiting factors that had to be taken into account. These included the extent of the developers' land ownership and the existence of travel routes, as well as military and trade considerations. No doubt, land ownership imposed the single most restraining factor on the site selection process in colonial Ireland. The larger the land holdings, the greater the range of potential sites open to the town developer.

In terms of location, most of the new towns were sited on river edge locations as these offered the potential for shipping, an important consideration in the site selection process. Sites on river estuaries were particularly advantageous as their location offered a combination of both strategic and commercial advantages. Control of the river itself could be guarded and maintained, and at the same time the site offered the possibility for a sea port from which international trade could be undertaken. It is not surprising, then, that under Norman direction a fresh array of coastal towns such as Carlingford in County Louth, Carrickfergus in County Antrim and Youghal in County Cork made their appearance around the perimeter of the country, adding to the older Viking coastal system.

Where coastal sites were not available, up-river locations were chosen. It is not without significance that, excluding the pre-Norman settlements, only a handful of the Norman towns, such Mullingar in County Westmeath, Naas in County Kildare and Nenagh in County Tipperary, were not connected directly with navigable rivers. The result of the choice of riverside locations was that most rivers acquired a string of towns along their banks. The river system of the Barrow, the Nore and the Suir, for example, acted like a corridor and had no fewer than thirteen Norman foundations spread out along the riverbanks (Fig.23).

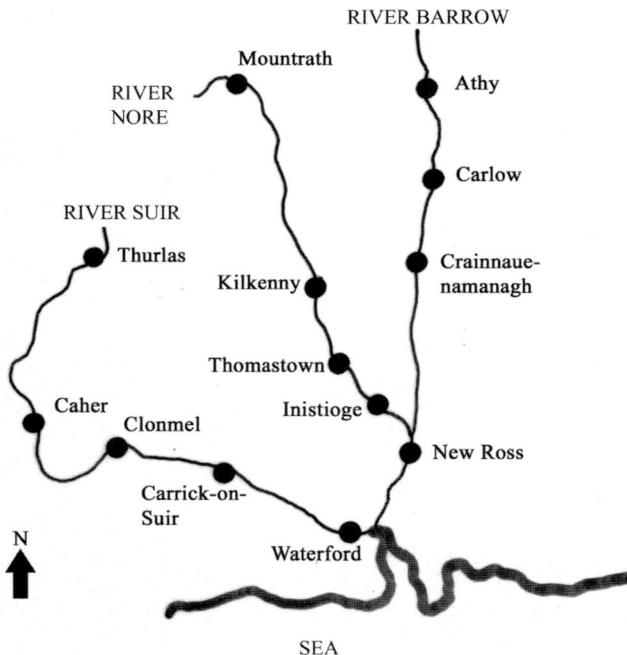

Fig.23: Colonial towns on the Barrow, Nore, and Suir river systems.

TOWN PLANNING

Throughout the medieval period, a range of standard planning components were used in the Irish colonial town planning process, all based on earlier English and Welsh practices. These included a town castle, the street plan, burgages, a market area, churches, town defences, and suburbs.

TOWN CASTLES

One of the earliest components of the new town to be laid in place was the town castle. It offered protection to the new settlement and acted as a base around which the town plan was laid out. Very often the plan was arranged so the castle took a position at the town edge, often in corner or waterfront positions. Here it formed a vital part of the town defences. The castles at Limerick (Fig.24) and Trim, for example, even today, dominate the river fronts of their respective towns. In contrast, a number of towns, such as Galway and Kells, had their castle placed in a central position within the town plan. A number of towns were laid out without a town castle, but these often had castles in their immediate vicinity. For example, the castles at Ardee in County Louth, and Callan and Thomastown in County Kilkenny, were each located a short distance from their respective town boundaries. Norman towns totally without castles are a rarity. Dundalk in County Louth, Kinsale in County Cork, and New Ross in County Wexford, were examples where it was probably felt that local military conditions were secure enough to dispense with a castle.

STREET LAYOUT

The street pattern of the colonial towns was essentially based on a combination of linear streets, which could be straight or curved, depending on the ground conditions. A small number of towns such as Nenagh in County Tipperary were laid out on a cross-linear plan, while others

Fig.24: King John's Castle, Limerick, County Limerick.

such as Athboy in County Meath were given a 'Y' or forked plan. In the case of the larger towns, such as Carlingford in County Louth and New Ross in County Wexford, the streets were laid out on an irregular grid pattern. Whether these grid layouts were part of a master plan or whether these town layouts grew in stages is uncertain.

BURGAGES

Although it was the street pattern that provided the framework for most Norman towns, it was the sub-division of the blocks into individual building plots or 'burgages', which formed the most important elements. The burgage was the basic property unit within the medieval town. Thus, the laying out of the burgage pattern was one of the earliest tasks of the town founder. Afterwards, it was the tenant or 'burgess' who was responsible for the building of his house on the plot, usually at the head, fronting the street, while the back-land was used for gardens or orchards. Characteristically, the burgages were long and narrow, and were arranged side by side along the streets and market places. It is interesting to note that the plot boundaries of a large number of Irish towns, such as those at Kilkenny in County Kilkenny and Loughrea in County Galway are extremely long living and can be traced back to those laid out during the Norman period.

SETTLERS

There were two attractions for the Norman landowner in building towns. Firstly, the new towns acted as administrative and military centres for controlling and defending the newly acquired lands and at the same time they produced income to the landowner in the form of rents. These town rents were generated by leasing the burgages to the Norman settlers, who arrived in the new colony from all across Britain and Europe and paid a yearly rent of one shilling a year to the town owner. In this way the rents provided a significant income to the land owner and provided a loyal garrison to defend the landowner's territory in times of danger. Information on what attracted the settlers to the new Irish colony is uncertain, but it is worth remembering that this same period saw a significant population rise in Britain and Continental Europe and this, combined with the privileges of town citizenship, such as fixed rents and right of trial before equals, probably made the prospects of moving to the new Irish colony an attractive proposition.

TOWN FABRIC

Each new colonial town was given its own parish church to cater for the spiritual needs of the new colonists. As in the case of the town castles, parish churches can be found in several locations within the plan of most towns. Judging by the numbers, it would seem that the parish church site most preferred by the Norman town builders was a perimeter one, such as can be found in Clonmel in County Tipperary and Youghal in County Cork. That is, a site with one or more of its boundaries forming part of the town wall. In other cases, the church was built in a central position, such as at Ardee and Dundalk in County Louth. In contrast to the general trend, a small number of towns had their churches located outside the town walls. Amongst these were Buttevant in County Cork, Navan in County Meath and Thurles in County Tipperary. Why these churches came to be positioned outside the town is unknown, but the answer may lie in some form of pre-Norman parish arrangements. As well as parish churches, most of the colonial towns possessed one or more religious houses such as the Augustinian, Dominican and Franciscan orders. These religious communities were not only centres of worship, but also places of learning and medical care, and they were placed randomly around their respective towns.

Significant though the churches and religious houses were, it was the housing that made up the bulk of the Norman town architecture. Most of the colonial town housing was made up of wooden framed buildings. Today, not a single example survives, although the appearance and form of these houses can be judged from eighteenth- and nineteenth-century illustrations (Fig.25). The fifteenth century did, however, see the construction of a number of small stone castles, or urban tower houses, a number of which still survive, notable in Ardee (Fig.26) and Carlingford, both in County Louth.

Fig.25: Wooden framed house, Dublin, c.1613.

Fig.26: Fifteenth-century town house, Ardee, County Louth.

TOWN MARKET

Once a town had been successfully established and settled, the next stage in the town development came into operation. This was the establishment of a town market. If a town was to succeed, it needed a market, to sell both its produce and that of the surrounding lands. In order to hold a market, however, a town required a market charter and this had to be secured from the Crown for a payment.

The market place tended to be linear, rectangular, or wedge-shaped in layout. The linear form of market place was by far the most commonly used. This consisted of a simple linear market space accommodated in a wide sector of the principal street. Even today, this form of linear market place remains the dominant feature of a large number of the Norman towns such as Ardee. A less commonly used form of market area was the rectangular market place. Here the market space was achieved by laying out a formal market square such as the Market Place in Carlingford. A more common form of the Norman market area was the wedge-shape. This was generally incorporated into the angle of the forked street plan. Cashel, Fethard and Thurles, all in County Tipperary, offer the clearest examples of this form, although Cashel has suffered a loss of its original space through 'market colonisation'. This refers to the reduction in the original market area from encroachment. That is where the market stall holders gradually acquired property rights, which allowed them to build permanent stalls in the market place. Eventually, these structures evolved into small town blocks that reduced the original space of the market area.

TOWN CHARTER

Like the market charter, the town charter was usually issued by the Crown. However, in the colonial conditions of Norman Ireland, this right was often practiced by the Norman lords themselves, particularly in the period up to the fifteenth century. The larger towns like Dublin, Cork, Limerick, and Waterford received their charters from the King, while smaller towns like Dungarvan, Wexford, Kells, Trim, Kilkenny, and New Ross held their charters from the Norman barons.

TOWN WALLING

The final and most representative stage in the Norman town development process was the construction of the town wall. These walls protected the citizens in times of danger, controlled the flow of goods in and out of the town, and added prestige and status to the settlement. The practice of walling the Norman towns was widespread, with large stretches of wall surviving in Athenry in County Galway, Carlingford in County Louth, and Fethard in County Tipperary (Fig.27). Elsewhere, some thirty colonial towns, such as Cashel in County Tipperary, still possess the partial remains of their walls in various states of preservation.

Most town walls were given wall towers. These were usually positioned at the corner or weak points in the wall circuit. The former were by far the most common, although intermediate towers were to be found in the larger centres such as Dublin, Limerick, Waterford, and Athenry. Even more significant than the towers were the town gates. These were the weakest point in the town defences and were often given the added protection of a defended gate-house. In its simplest form, this consisted of a simple tower with the gateway passing through the structure at ground level. In more elaborate examples, the gate house was fronted by an outer tower, or barbican, and drawbridge. Almost thirty medieval town gates survive intact throughout Ireland, and within this group are to be found a whole range of gate structures, varying in scale from the massive barbican at St Laurence's Gate in Drogheda, County Louth (Fig.28) to the elementary North Gate of Fethard (Fig.29).

Outside the town wall, a further line of defence frequently existed, in the form of a town moat or ditch. The riverside location of most of the Irish towns such as Dublin, Kilkenny and New Ross, provided a natural moat and this was frequently supplemented by a man-made trench, dug around the outside of the town walling. The practice of walling the colonial towns seems to have begun in about 1234 and continued up to the sixteenth century and beyond. The cost of the wall and its ongoing maintenance was financed through murage grants. These were charters issued by the Crown that authorised a town to raise the necessary funding by imposing a tax on persons entering through the town gates.

SUBURBS

In colonial Ireland, as elsewhere in medieval Europe, a large number of the towns acquired significant suburbs outside the town walls. These usually followed a linear street arrangement prompted, perhaps, by the road lines which stretched outwards from the town gates. The dating of these suburbs is often uncertain, but the early seventeenth century maps of Kilmallock in County Limerick (Fig.30) and Ardee indicate extensive suburban developments which even incorporated their own outer town gates. Occasionally such suburbs were situated on the river banks directly opposite the main town, usually on the far side of the town bridges. Enniscorthy in County Wexford as well as Carrick-on-Suir and Clonmel in County Tipperary, for example, all developed typical bridge-head suburbs of this form. In the case of the larger towns, such as Kilkenny and Limerick, such suburban developments were very substantial indeed and were eventually incorporated into their respective towns by means of an extension of the town wall system.

Fig.27: Town Wall, Fethard, County Tipperary.

Fig.28: Barbican, St Laurence's Gate, Drogheda, County Louth.

Fig.29: North Gate, Fethard, County Tipperary.

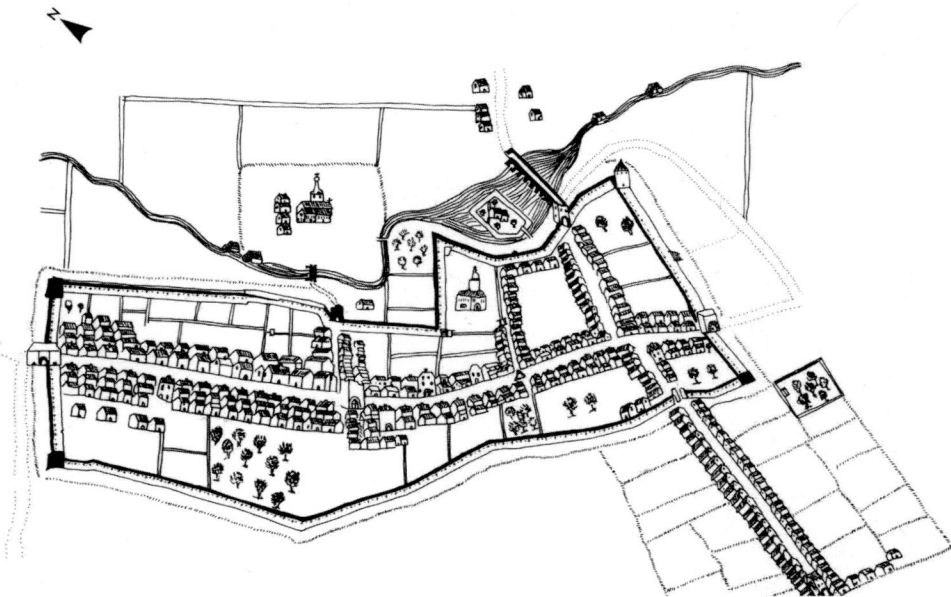

Fig.30: 1610 map of Kilmallock, County Limerick.

THE COLONIAL TOWN

Despite the use of standard planning elements, the interiors of most of the Norman towns differed considerably. A review of all the colonial towns lies outside the scope of this guide. However, a number of examples give a general idea of how the individual Norman towns developed and progressed. These include the promoted centres of Waterford and Kilkenny, and the new towns of Ardee, Fethard, Kilmallock, Drogheda, and Athenry.

WATERFORD

In Waterford, the colonial town development took the form of an extensive new sector that was added on the western edge of the earlier triangular shaped Viking town. This consisted of the major north/south line of Barron Strand Street and John's Street. This was narrow for most of its length except where it broadened out into a wedge-shaped market areas at either end. From Figure 31, it can be seen that the two sectors of the town were linked by means of St Patrick Street, which acted both as a continuation of the original Viking axis and as cross street to the new Norman sector. In addition to the main axis, the colonial layout included a range of irregular secondary streets – all of which were lined by burgages. In this way, the new colonial sector stretched southwards in a block from the bank of the River Suir to the St John's River.

The fabric of the Norman Waterford included the parish churches of St Patrick and St Michael, as well as St Stephen's church and hospital and St John's Priory. The defences of the town began in around 1225. This included the strengthening of the original Viking walls, including the dividing wall between the old and new sectors. The new sector was also walled so that on completion the entire city was enclosed by a continuous system of stone walls, wall towers and defended gate-houses. Today a significant stretch of the eastern town wall survives and includes a number of the wall towers (Fig.32).

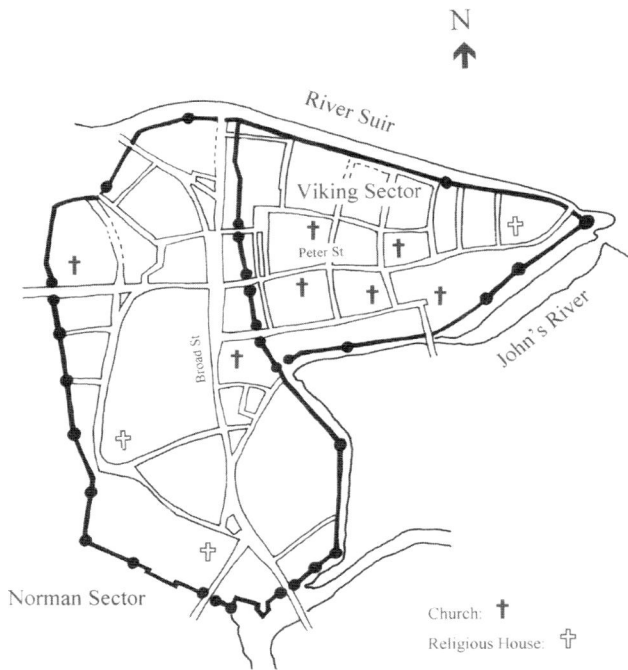

N

River Suir

Viking Sector

Peter St

Broad St

John's River

Norman Sector

Church: †
Religious House: ⌖

Fig.31: Plan of Norman Waterford, County Waterford.

Fig.32: Town wall, Waterford, County Waterford.

KILKENNY

Kilkenny dates from about the sixth century, with the establishment of two Early Christian settlements, Irishtown and Donaghmore, which were subsequently developed in several phases by the Normans. In its pre-colonial form, the Irishtown settlement was positioned on a low hill, immediately north of a point where the small River Bregagh joined the main stream of the River Nore. Here the layout consisted of a double enclosure with the present cathedral grounds occupying the original inner core. Outside of this the curve of Vicar Street, Dean Street, Thomas Street, and Church Lane mark the outer enclosure (Fig.33). A little over a kilometre southwards, Donaghmore was laid out in a similar fashion, although today the circular layout arrangement has almost vanished, except for the remains of a graveyard and some adjacent curved property boundaries.

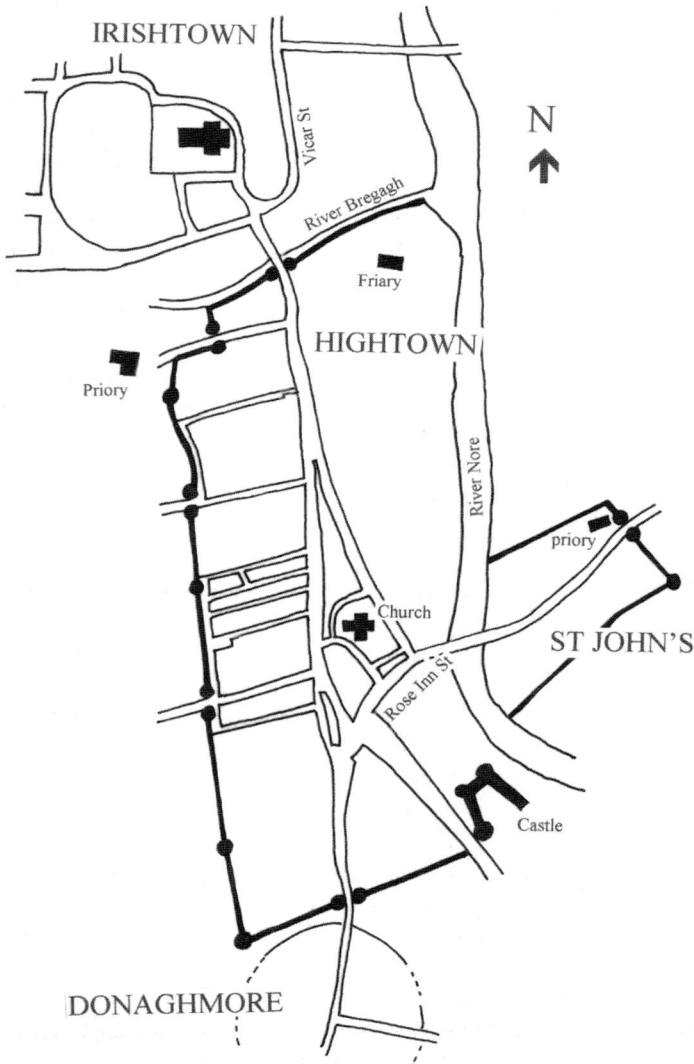

IRISHTOWN

Vicar St

N

River Bregagh

Friary

HIGHTOWN

Priory

River Nore

priory

Church

ST JOHN'S

Rose Inn St

Castle

DONAGHMORE

Fig.33: Plan of Norman Kilkenny, County Kilkenny.

By 1173, Richard de Clare, often referred to as Strongbow, had occupied this area and it was probably he who started work on the promotion of the settlement in a position that lay between the two Early Christian sites. The new development was called Hightown, and consisted initially of two main elements, the town castle and the street layout. In 1173, the first phase in the colonial development took place with the building of Kilkenny Castle, directly north-east of Donaghmore. Here it commanded both the earlier settlements and a bend in the Nore. The next stage in the development consisted of the laying out of an extended wedge-shaped street which stretched northwards from the northern boundary of Donaghmore.

Within this arrangement, three secondary streets were laid out perpendicular to the wedge, and these led to a series of gates along the western edge of the new town. At the same time, the new streets were lined with burgages. In addition, or perhaps later, the castle grounds were enclosed by Rose Inn Street, which stretched in a curve from the southern town gate, along the base of the wedge, and finished at a new bridge over the Nore. North of the castle, the parish church of St Mary was placed centrally in the wide wedge-shaped market space.

De Clare died in 1176 and the lands eventually passed to his son-in-law, William Marshall, who issued the first charter to the town in 1207. In the same year, Marshall acquired a tract of church land at the northern end of the wedge and extended the town northwards as far as the River Bregagh. Following this, the final stage of the colonial development took place when the St John's suburb was laid out on the east bank of the Nore. The plan of the suburb consisted of a single street that lined up with the town bridge and probably dates from the period following the foundation of the Augustinian priory there in 1211. At some period, the wedge-shaped market area was colonised and, in around 1250, work began on the town wall which ultimately enclosed Hightown and Irishtown. These were physically attached, but independently operated and administered

The Norman fabric survival in Kilkenny is extensive and includes a number of stretches of the western town wall (Fig.34), two wall towers and the remains of Abbey Gate. The ruins of the Franciscan Friary in Hightown and Augustinian Friary in St John's suburb also survive, as well as the St Mary's Parish Church and restored Dominican Priory (Fig.35).

FETHARD

The development of Fethard in County Tipperary dates from around 1185, when the territory was granted to Philip of Worcester, although twenty years later it came into the ownership of William de Braose. The town plan is focused on a wedge-shaped principal street, Main Street, which crosses the town from east to west, parallel to the Clashawley River (Fig.36). Despite its small size the development of the town is extremely complex. The extended wedge shaped Main Street acted as the market area, at the southern side of which St John's parish church was built. Five gates enter the town: one from the west, one from the north, two from the east, and one from the south. The western approach to the town was via a bridge over the river; and at the far end of Main Street, Barrack Street, Burke Street and Watergate Street were laid in a dog-leg fashion at an angle to the wedge-shaped market area. In addition, Sparagoulea and the curved Chapel Lane led indirectly northwards from Main Street.

The main colonial feature of the town today, apart from the street layout, is the almost total survival of the town wall, including two wall towers, on which work began in about 1292 (Fig.37). Unfortunately, all the gates, with the exception of North Gate, have now disappeared. Inside the town walls, parts of the Holy Trinity parish church still survive as well as do fifteenth-century tower houses and a seventeenth-century market house.

Fig. 34: Town wall, Kilkenny, County Kilkenny.

Fig. 35: Dominical Priory, Kilkenny, County Kilkenny.

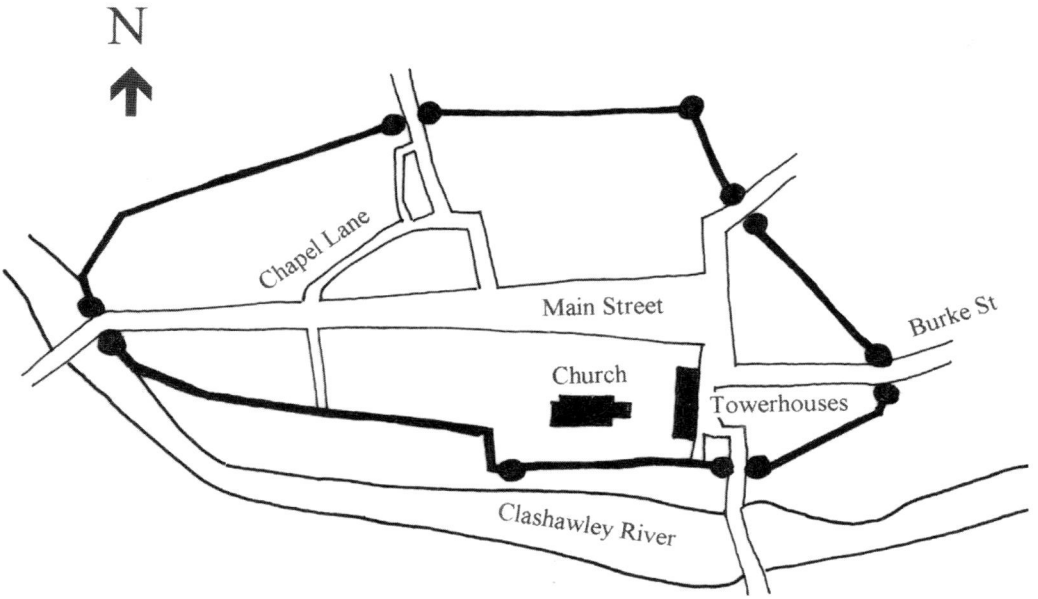

Above: Fig.36: Plan of Norman Fethard, County Tipperary.

Left: Fig.37: Town wall, Fethard, County Tipperary.

KILMALLOCK

The town of Kilmallock in County Limerick seems to have been established on a green field site, on the south bank of the River Loobagh, by Desmond Fitzgerald, in the early years of the thirteenth century. The foundation date is uncertain, but a market charter was granted as early as 1221. The town seems to have developed in four stages, which included an initial cross-linear plan, two eastern extensions and a suburb (Fig.38). First a cross-linear street pattern, with the parish church in the extreme northern corner, was laid out beside the river. The line of Sarsfield Avenue and Lord Edward Street follows a north-eastern line, while the cross axis consists of Emmet and Wolf Tone Streets. At this early stage, the town boundary probably lay along the north-western line of the church grounds and in a continuation of this line southwards.

North-west of this, two abrupt changes in the town wall circuit suggest that the town expanded westwards in two stages. The first of these consisted of a short extension of Sarsfield Avenue. This seems to have terminated at the line of the town castle. In fact, the castle probably began as gateway to this expanded area. North-west of this again, the second expansion consisted of a further continuation of the line of Sarsfield Avenue.

The final development stage took the form of a single suburban street, the continuation southwards of the line of Emmet Street. The map of 1610 shows the sector un-walled, but protected by its own gate-house (Fig.30). All traces of the suburb have now vanished – if indeed, it ever existed. In terms of fabric, a considerable section of the town wall still survives (Fig.39) as does the town castle (Fig.40), Blossom Gate (Fig.41) and the ruins of the Dominican Friary, on the north side of the river.

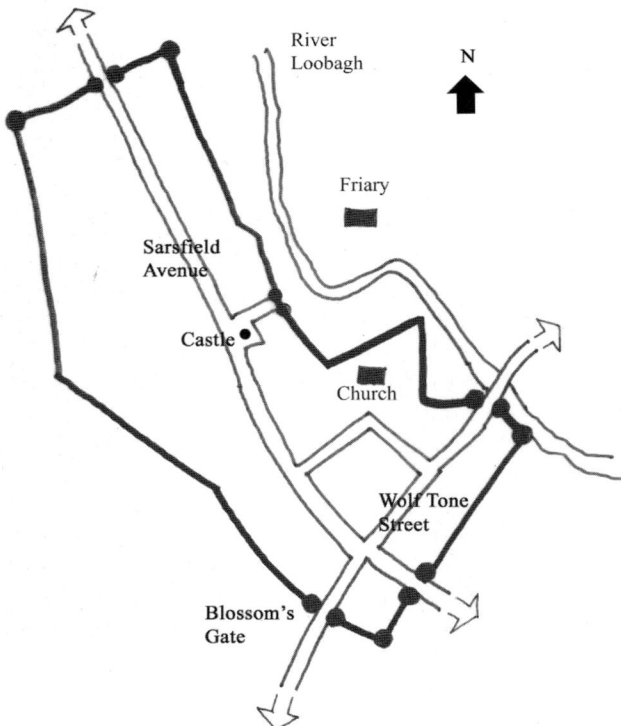

Fig.38: Plan, Norman Kilmallock, County Limerick.

Fig.39: Town wall, Kilmallock, County Limerick.

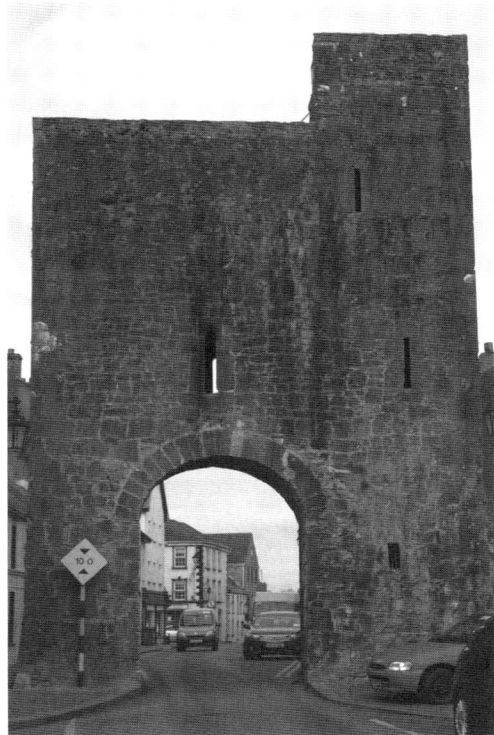

Above left: Fig.40: Town castle, Kilmallock, County Limerick.

Above right: Fig.41: Blossom Gate, Kilmallock, County Limerick.

ARDEE

The territory around Ardee in County Louth was granted to Gilbert Pipard by Prince John in about 1185. Shortly after this, Pipard erected an earth-built castle, a motte, on the south bank of the River Dee. He then proceeded to lay out his new town on the far side of the river, about a kilometre upstream. The town developed fast and in 1191 it was necessary to build St Mary's parish church. In its initial form, the town was laid out the simple linear plan, the line of Main Street and Castle Street. This stretched northward between the bridge over the river and Head Gate (Fig.42). The street was flanked with the usual burgages and the parish church was positioned midway along the street on the east side.

At this period, the town must have been prosperous and, like Kilmallock, it was decided to increase its size by expanding eastwards, with access to the new area provided by three new streets: Markethouse Lane, Lamb's Lane, and Tisdale Street. Following this, the three new streets were linked by a system of irregular lanes. Finally the entire town, including the extension, was enclosed by a stone wall. Unfortunately, the expanded sector of the town failed to prosper and the expanded area seems to have lain undeveloped until the arrival of the railway in the nineteenth century.

Curiously the suburb, Irish Street, on the north side of the town, did prosper. This had its origins in the development of burgages along the northern approach road to the town, immediately outside Head Gate. Such was the success of the suburb that at some period it warranted the construction of its own outer North Gate. However, like the Kilmallock suburb, a date for the construction of Irish Street is unknown. Today, nothing remains of Ardee's town walls, although the town has four surviving examples of its medieval architecture. These include two-century tower houses (Fig.26), sections of the parish Church on Main Street, and the ruins of the College Chapel in a back lane directly behind the parish church grounds.

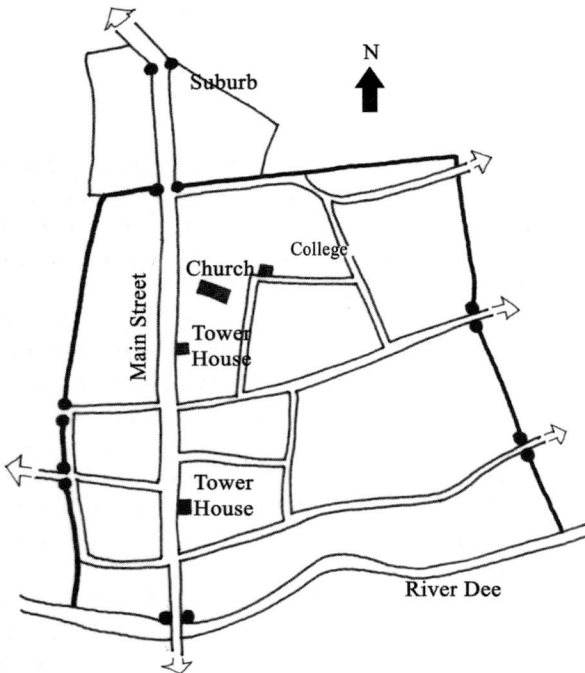

Fig.42: Plan of Norman Ardee, County Louth.

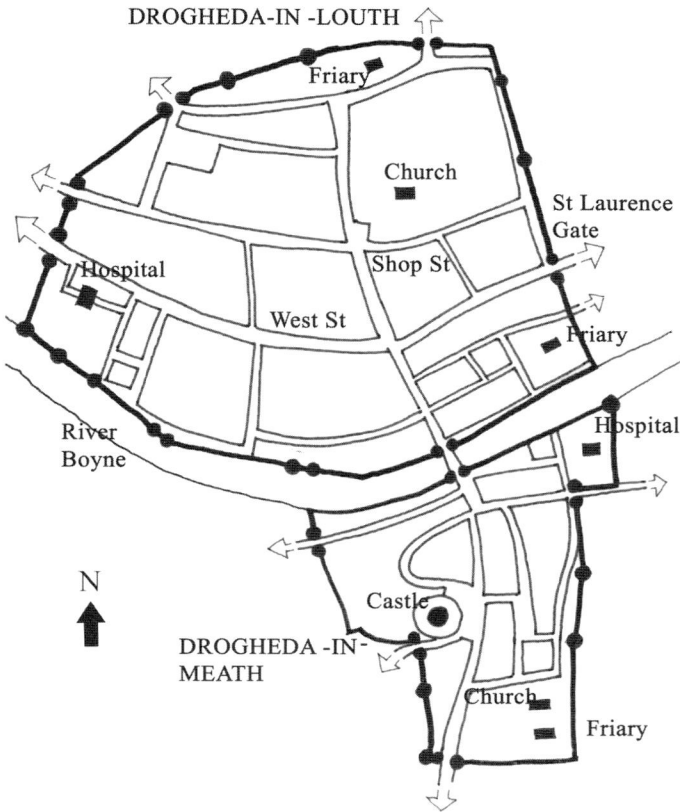

DROGHEDA-IN-LOUTH

Friary

Church

St Laurence
Gate

Hospital

Shop St

West St

Friary

River
Boyne

Hospital

N

Castle

DROGHEDA-IN-
MEATH

Church

Friary

Fig.43: Plan of Norman
Drogheda, County Louth.

DROGHEDA

Norman Drogheda consisted initially of a pair of totally independent towns: Drogheda-in-Meath and Drogheda-in-Louth. The two towns faced one another across the River Boyne, and were linked together by a single bridge. Drogheda-in-Meath lay on the southern, County Meath side of the river and Drogheda-in-Louth on the northern, County Louth side. It was only in 1412 that the two towns were merged into a single unit (Fig.43).

Drogheda-in-Meath was established towards the end of the twelfth century, when Hugh de Lacy built a motte-and-bailey on the south side of the River Boyne about eight kilometres upstream from the sea, and followed this with the laying out of his complex new town. The motte was built on the edge of a high bank that overlooked a flat riverside area below. In an unusual move, the new town was laid out on both the upper and lower levels. On the upper level, an irregular grid of streets was laid out on the east side of the motte, with the central street, Duleek Street, dropping steeply from the high level to the lower level, so as to line up with the bridge. The grid layout centred on a rectangular market place, south of which the parish church and a Carmelite Friary were established.

Below this, the lower level of the town was laid out on a simple grid. This included a number of linear streets arranged parallel to the river, a riverside quay, and the Hospital of St James. The overall plan of the de Lacy town therefore consisted of an L-shaped river fronted town on two levels, with de Lacy's motte in the angle of the L.

A foundation date for Drogheda-in-Louth is uncertain; but it probably dates from around the same period as Drogheda-in-Meath. The land here was granted to Bertrand de Vernon and it was probably he who began work on the development. The de Vernon town was much larger that Drogheda-in-Meath and consisted of an irregular grid, laid out on the gently sloping north bank of the river. Shop Street and St Peter Street stretch northwards from the town bridge, while the cross axis of West Street and St Laurence Street runs parallel to the gentle bend in the river. Within the street network, the parish church was positioned on the east side of St Peter Street. In addition, the town had three religious houses: the Franciscan Friary, near the east edge of the town, the Friary of Fratres Cruciferi on the opposite side of the town, and the Dominican Friary at the northern edge.

In 1234, work started on the town wall and when it was completed it fully enclosed both of the town sectors. This gave the combined towns a defensive system of walls, wall towers and defended town gates. These included four major gates in Drogheda-in-Meath and about five major gates in the northern counterpart. Today the Norman town plan in both towns remains much as it was during the Norman period, but only the occasional remnants of the religious houses and the town walls survive. The one exception is the splendid barbican at the St Laurence Street Gate which survives intact (Fig.28).

ATHENRY

Meiler de Bermingham was granted lands around Athenry in County Galway, during the early part of the thirteenth century. There, he built a strong castle beside the narrow River Clareen and immediately south of this he laid out the new town on both sides of the river. Curiously, most of the town is concentrated in the west side of the river and consists of an irregular grid with a central triangular market area (Fig.44). The parish church lies directly north of the market place and fronts onto Chapel Street.

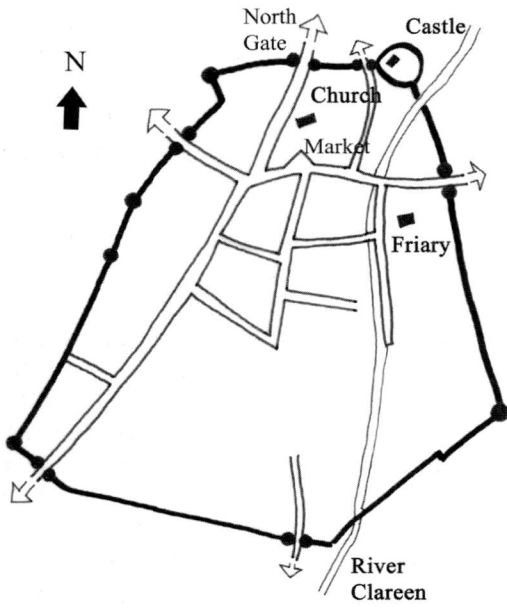

Fig.44: Plan of Norman Athenry, County Galway.

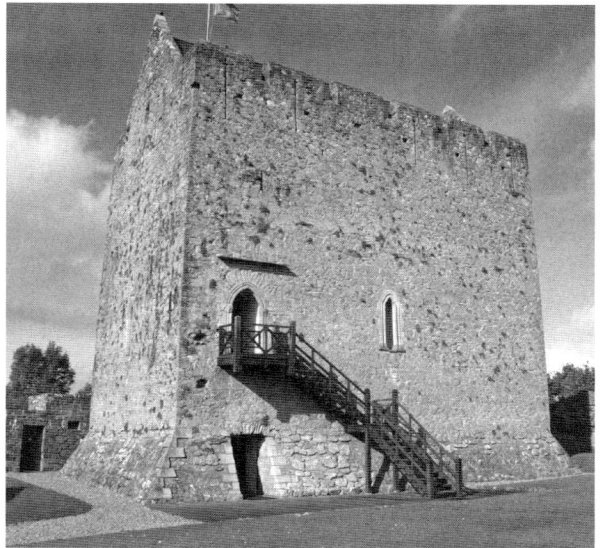

Above left: Fig.45: North Gate, Athenry, County Galway.

Above right: Fig.46: Castle, Athenry, County Galway.

In contrast to the western sector of the town, little development seems to have taken place on the east bank of the river, except for the Dominican Friary and at this stage the line of Cross Street marked the southern edge of the town. At some later period, it was decided to extend the town southwards, presumably to cater for potential growth. As was the case with Ardee, the original town and the extended area was walled, but expansion proved unsuccessful. In fact, there was a proposal in 1583 to divide the successful northern sector of the town from the undeveloped southern sectors by the building of a dividing wall – although it is uncertain whether this wall was ever built.

Apart from the street pattern, the outstanding medieval feature of Norman Athenry is the surviving fabric. This includes the extensive circuit of the town wall, the wall towers, the powerful North Gate (Fig.45), the extensively restored town castle (Fig.46), and the ruined parish church and friary.

DECLINE OF THE COLONY

The middle of the thirteenth century found that the Normans had reached the most westerly parts of Ireland, and by 1245 the coastal areas of Donegal and Kerry were under colonial occupation. By this time, however, the Norman drive had reached its maximum, and almost immediately afterwards it faltered. Even at this point, the Norman conquest of the island, as a whole, had never been completed. During the forward thrust of the conquest, large pockets of territory had been bypassed, and by about 1300 the native Gaelic chieftains began a vigorous counter attack from these areas. This gradually pushed the colonial frontiers slowly back eastwards across the country. The coronation of Edward Bruce as King of Ireland, in 1316, and his subsequent military expeditions through the country, spelled disaster, and added to the colony's decline. But even more misfortune was to follow; two further factors combined to undermine the colonial structure: the weakness of the Norman population and the Black Death.

Despite the expectations and efforts of the Norman overlords, only a relatively small number of colonists were attracted to the new territories. In effect, the colony was never settled with a sufficient number of settlers to allow for the establishment of any long-term Norman presence. This was particularly so in the northern and western areas of the country. The arrival of the Black Death, in the middle of the fourteenth century, inflicted the final disaster. In the autumn of 1348, the plague appeared in the ports of Drogheda and Howth, from where it spread out across the country, attacking the population, particularly those in the towns.

As a result of these events, the close of the fourteenth century witnessed the flight of many colonists from the country, further reducing the population. By this time, the effective territory of the colony had been reduced to the area of the Pale, an area of land that lay around Dublin. Outside of this, the country was under the control of a mixture of Gaelic chieftains and Anglo-Irish lords, each bearing various levels of allegiances to the Crown. Scattered throughout this complex situation were the towns, many of which ultimately fell to native Irish attack. Roscommon and Athlone had been lost by 1355, as had Coleraine and Sligo, and in 1400 Armagh was recorded as being under Gaelic control. By 1550, Loughrea was in ruins, although the nearby towns of Galway and Athenry managed to hold out as centres of colonial power and influence.

As the colony declined, the weaker towns fell to attack, while the stronger centres patiently sat out the middle ages, safe behind the protection of their walls. Politically, these towns were outside all but nominal Royal authority and they became almost totally independent. In this way, they acted as successful centres of trade, and as loyal outposts of Norman, and subsequent English influence. The native Irish seem to have lacked either the resources, or the military strength, to capture the larger and better fortified towns. This unstable state of affairs continued in Ireland right through the medieval period, and it was not until the assumption by Henry VIII of the title 'King of Ireland' in 1541, that the situation was finally brought to a close. The high point of Irish town foundation had passed.

The effects of the Norman town builders were extensive and had a lasting impact on the development of the Irish town network, in terms of numerical strength, distribution, town planning, and fabric survival. Over sixty new towns were established and survived the middle ages, and today these make up the greater portion of the Irish town network. The pre-conquest Viking towns of Dublin, Cork, Waterford, and Limerick dominate the Irish town system, but a number of the purely Norman centres such as Drogheda, Dundalk and Galway have succeeded in taking their places in the upper levels of this system. In reality, the Normans were responsible for creating the major part of the Irish national town network.

In terms of continuity, the resilience of the town plans laid in place during the colonial period is remarkable. In fact, so successful and long lasting are these plan-forms that, with the exception of Cork, Dublin and Limerick, the town cores put into place by the Normans still function as such today – despite nearly seven hundred years of changing fortunes.

Within the Norman towns the survival rate of medieval fabric is high, as the great bulk of the colonial towns offer at least some remains of their medieval architecture. These include town castles, churches, religious houses, and stretches of town defences. Indeed, it is the rare town which does not contain at least one physical reminder of its Norman past. Athenry, Carlingford, and Fethard, to single out a few examples, have large parts of their town wall defences intact. In other cases, such as Athenry, Cahir, Limerick, and Trim the town castles have been successfully restored and are open for visitors. In the case of religious buildings, most towns have the remains of at least a single example such as a parish church, abbey or friary. Mullingar and Navan alone are unique in the absence of any surviving medieval fabric.

FIVE

THE PLANTATION

1550 – 1650

THE PLANTATION

The Plantation town-building movement represents the fourth phase in the development of the Irish town system. This movement began around the middle of the sixteenth century, lasted for about one hundred years, and saw the creation of a fresh wave of new towns across the Irish landscape, particularly in the northern half of the country. By this period, English control in Ireland was confined mainly to the Pale and to a number of the Norman towns such as Drogheda, Cork, Galway, Kilkenny, and Limerick. During this time, the English monarchy decided to bring Ireland under their control and from about 1550 onwards, they launched a series of campaigns to achieve this. These included military conquests, the taking of lands from the Gaelic lords, and the plantation of these confiscated lands with English and Scottish settlers. For this reason, this period in Irish history is generally referred to as the Plantation.

One aspect of the Plantation period that stands out is the creation of a range of new towns to help secure these newly conquered lands. In effect, this process was almost a replay of the Norman town-building operations of the earlier period. As in the earlier period, the Plantation town development process followed the same stages used by the Norman town builders: land acquisition, site selection, town planning, the introduction of settlers, the building of the town fabric, the issuing of a market and town charter, and the construction of town defences. There were, however, a number of small changes in the techniques used.

LAND ACQUISITION

As was the case in the Norman period, once an area was taken into English control, the process of plantation and town development began. One of the major policy differences between the Norman town development and that of the Plantation was the financing arrangements. During the late sixteenth century, the English crown had acquired large tracts of land across the country through conquest. The proposal was to secure these lands by settling them with loyal settlers. This was achieved by granting the lands to individuals called 'undertakers' such as Sir Nicholas Bagnal in County Down and Richard Boyle in County Cork. These undertakers were obliged to secure the lands, establishing new towns, and populate them with loyal settlers – all from their own resources. The financial returns to the undertakers came from the property rents imposed on the settlers, much as it was during the Norman period.

SITE SELECTION

The Plantation site selection process was similar to that used in the Norman times, and was concentrated in two areas of activity. These included the promotion of established centres and the foundation of new towns. Birr in County Offaly, Castlebar in County Mayo and Ennis in County Clare, for example, were all medieval foundations which were promoted during the Plantation period. In the case of new foundations, river and coastal sites, such as Belfast in County Antrim, Coleraine in County Derry, Newry in County Down and Portarlington in County Laois, were selected.

TOWN PLANNING

Plantation town-planning designs had their roots in the early European Renaissance period, where the fifteenth and sixteenth centuries saw considerable advances in town planning ideas. These were based on ancient Greece and Rome models and included wide streets to accommodate traffic, the provision of public open spaces, the use of grid street patterns, and the requirements for town defences. The layout of Palma Nova in Italy will, for example, illustrate the form these sixteenth-century towns took. The layout here was designed by Scamozzi and work began in about 1590. The internal layout consists of eighteen streets, arranged in a radial grid fitted into a nine-sided figure (Fig.47). There was a large central open space and six smaller ones, distributed around the grid. The town was protected by a wall, outside of which lay a moat. A striking feature of the town wall was the inclusion of nine bastions, one at each corner. The bastion was a commonly used arrow-shaped wall tower that projected out from the main line of the wall. It provided a platform for artillery and gave the town wall a distinctive star-shaped outline.

It was from Palma Nova, and towns like it, that the Plantation town builders drew much of their layout plans. These included the use of grid street plans, central market places and star-shaped wall defences. In addition, the Plantation town builders incorporated many of the features used previously by the Normans. These included a town castle, burgages, a market area, and a site for a church, as well as the use of town wall and market charters. The street pattern of the larger Plantation towns like Coleraine and Derry followed a grid pattern, while the arrangements in more modest towns were often linear or cross-linear in form. The burgages continued to be laid out in the form of long narrow strips, much as they had been in Norman times.

In contrast to the Norman period, a number of formal town plans survive from the Plantation period. The 1581 map of Roscommon in County Roscommon shows the Norman castle, beside which the proposed new town was laid out. This consisted of a rectangular pattern of linear street with a market place to one side. The town walls included two semicircular bastions and a rectangular corner tower, outside of which was a moat – supplied with water from the adjacent lake (Fig.48). There is, however, little evidence that this plan was ever implemented, as the present town lies directly south of Roscommon Castle.

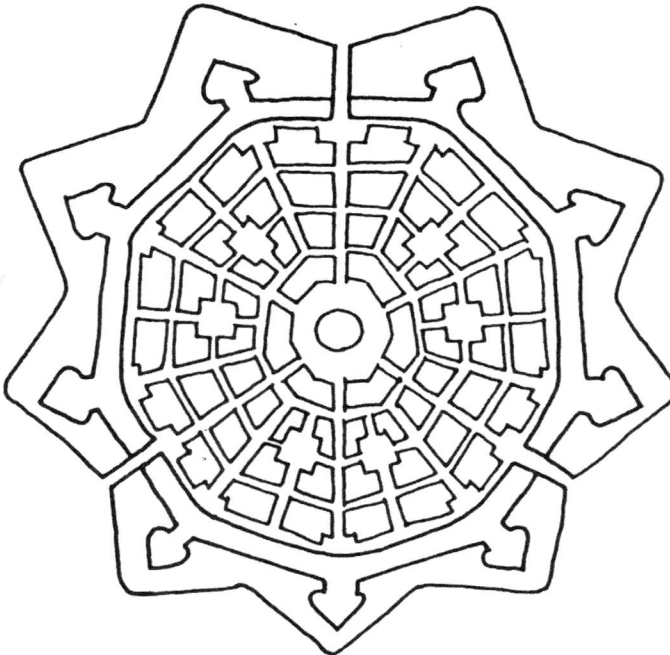

Fig.47: Plan, Palma Nova, Italy.

The early seventeenth-century map of Sir Edward Blaney's new town of Monaghan also offers an idea of the typical approach to Plantation town planning (Fig.49). The town houses are shown, arranged in a cross-linear form, with an off-centre market place. Directly north of the market is a large enclosure, inside of which is the town castle, behind which, a formal garden is laid out. The town wall encloses both the town and the castle grounds, and outside of this the moat is supplied from the adjacent lake. The wall has an arrow-shaped bastion at three of the corners, as well as two intermediate bastions. Curiously, the line of the town wall is broken at the south-east corner, where it abuts the lake. The map shows three gates but no arrangement seems to have been made for a church. It seems that the plan was not carried out in its totality, as it is difficult to reconcile the drawing with the present town layout. This is not an unusual situation, as the layout of Bandon, for example, differs from the original 1613 plan in terms of scale and street alignment. It is not certain why these changes were made, but they may have been forced by on-site ground conditions.

TOWN NETWORK

Like the Normans, the Plantation town developers first turned their attention to promoting the existing towns. The major established centres, such as Dublin, Drogheda, Carrickfergus, and Waterford, were strengthened and expanded. Following this, the new-town-building programme was implemented, particularly in the three major Plantation campaigns of Laois-Offaly, Munster and Ulster. In Counties Laois and Offaly, Dangan and Port Laois were built on the site of earlier forts; while in County Cork, Richard Boyle restored the towns of Lismore, Tallow and Youghal. It was, however, Ulster that experienced the most extensive wave of Plantation town development, where sixteen new towns were proposed in 1611. The pace of this programme was swift, and by 1641, all were established.

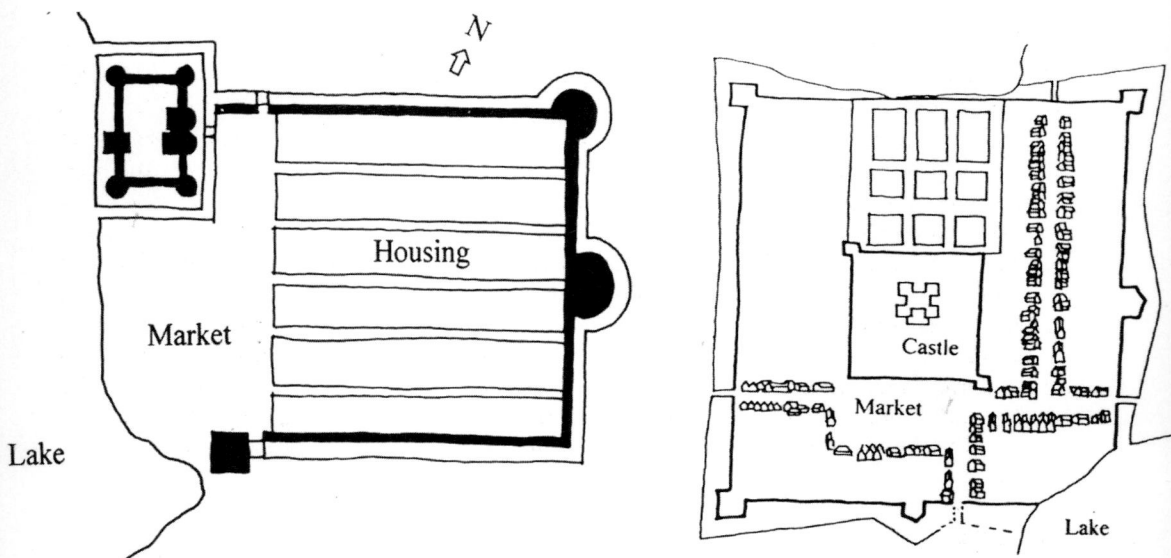

Above left: Fig.48: 1581 plan, Roscommon, County Roscommon.

Above right: Fig.49: Seventeenth-century plan, Monaghan, County Monaghan.

SETTLERS

The settlers who came to live in the Plantations towns were drawn principally from England and Scotland and were usually merchants, shopkeepers, and artisans. On arrival in their new towns, the settlers were allocated burgages which, like their medieval counterparts, they held under lease.

CHARTERS

Once a settlement advanced beyond its foundation stage, it was granted a market charter as had been the case in the Norman period. This was followed, rapidly in many cases, by the receipt of a town charter. Work was started on Belfast, for example, in 1603. A market was in existence by 1605, and a town charter was issued in 1613 – all within a ten year period. By the end of 1670, no fewer than twenty-eight new towns had been built in Ulster. Not all the new foundations, however, reached the stage of chartered towns. Omagh in County Tyrone, Tandragee in County Armagh, and Virginia in County Cavan, for example, failed to secure town charters, but nevertheless they went on to succeed as important market centres.

FABRIC

The survival of the fabric of the Plantation towns, as is the case with the Norman examples, is minimal and with the exception of a number of churches little has survived. The exception is Derry, that has retained its massive stone walls. Elsewhere, only the occasional fragments of a town wall survive such as the stretches at Carrickfergus in County Antrim and Jamestown in County Leitrim.

DEFENCES

The fort or castle was an important feature of most Plantation towns. Dangan and Port Laoise were created around forts, while Donegal and Lifford in County Donegal, Newry in County Down, and Monaghan in County Monaghan, for example, had defended houses and large courtyards incorporated into their defences. Town walls were an essential part of most Plantation towns and their construction was financed, as it had been in medieval times, by taxes raised through murage grants. In the larger examples, such as Bandon, Belfast, and Derry, the walls were of masonry construction, with defended gates, arrowhead bastions, and moats. Elsewhere, earth-built fortifications were the norm. Coleraine and Potrarlington, for example, had extensive earthen walls. Cheaper to build, but more expensive to maintain, the earth-built wall had one advantage. It could absorb cannon shot, thereby minimising the dangers from ricochet and splinters. This consideration aside, economic conditions usually forced the smaller centres such as Cavan in County Cavan and Gorey in County Wexford to rely on earthen defences. Taken together the components of the Plantation towns produced a town form that was similar in idea to the to the Norman towns, but different in its physical arrangement. Even today, the town plans of Newry, Derry, Coleraine, Portarlington, and Jamestown all demonstrate this.

NEWRY

One of the earliest available Plantation town plans is the 1570 drawing of Newry in County Down (Fig.50). The original site was granted to Nicholas Bagnal in about 1549, and work presumably started on the new town shortly afterwards, followed by the granting of a town charter in 1613. The map shows Bagnal's walled town, positioned on a ridge overlooking the River Newry. Internally,

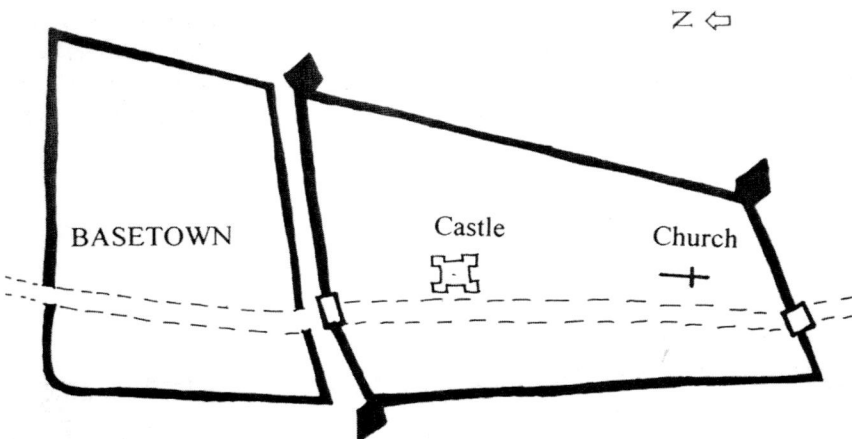

N ⟵

BASETOWN

Castle

Church

Fig. 50: 1570
plan, Newry,
County
Down.

the town is divided into two sectors: a rectangular 'Upper Town' and the lower, almost square suburb of 'Basetown'. Curiously, these were separated from one another by a narrow gap.

The map shows a single street, stretching through both sectors of the town. The Upper town seems to have been the most important and contained Bagnal's castle and the church, although both sectors show houses fronting onto the single street. The two sectors of the town seem to have been enclosed separately by an earthen wall and a moat in about 1550. The wall of the Upper Town is the more elaborate with arrow-head corner bastions and a pair of gate-houses. In contrast, Basetown seems to have been given more elementary defences. The division of the town, into two sectors, is a curious feature. The reasons for this are uncertain, but it may have been the result of a two-phased development.

DERRY

With the exception of the smaller Portarlington and Jamestown, the layout of Derry comes closest to the characteristic early Renaissance fortified towns, such as Palma Nova and Willemstad. The town has its origins in the Early Christian settlement of Derry, which was established in the sixth century, overlooking the River Foyle. The settlement survived throughout the medieval period and was taken over by Sir Henry Docwra in 1600, following which a fort was built and a new Plantation town followed. The new town received its market and town charter in 1603 and 1604 respectively. In 1613, the project was taken over by the City of London, or the Irish Society, and a completely new town was laid out. At this stage, the settlement was re-named Londonderry to mark the involvement of the City of London in the town development, although the original name Derry has now come into more general use.

Development of the new town was swift. In 1614, work began on the walling, and in 1622 a town plan was prepared which shows the work completed to that date (Fig. 51). The plan shows the town laid out in a gridiron form, with two major axes that cross at the central market square. The map shows the market house in the centre of the square and a fortified gatehouse, at the end of the each of the four main streets. In addition, the town's pre-Plantation castle and the medieval cathedral are shown in the north-west corner. In terms of defences, the map shows the town enclosed with a substantial wall outside of which is a moat. The wall circuit follows an approximate rectangular course with six arrowhead bastions placed around its circuit.

In terms of survival, the town's Plantation layout has experienced only minor modifications since the preparation of the 1622 plan. The castle has disappeared and the original cathedral was replaced by a new structure in the south-west corner in 1633. The city's stone walls are still in good repair, and have been amended only by alterations to the gate-houses and by the addition of three later gates and a number of minor towers (Fig. 52).

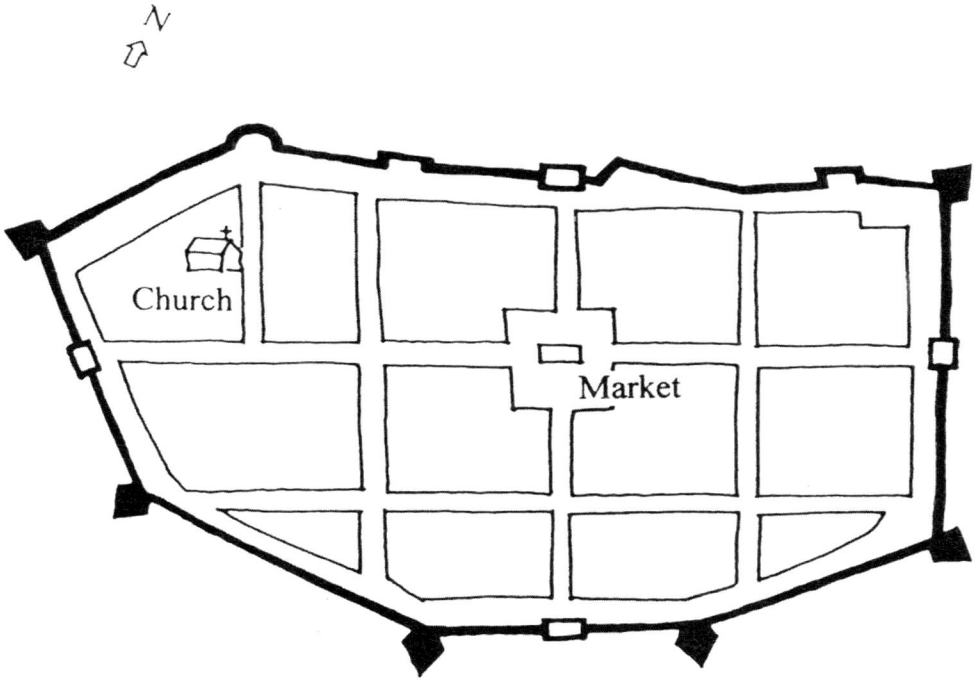

Fig. 51: 1622 plan, Derry, County Derry.

Fig. 52: Town wall, Derry, County Derry.

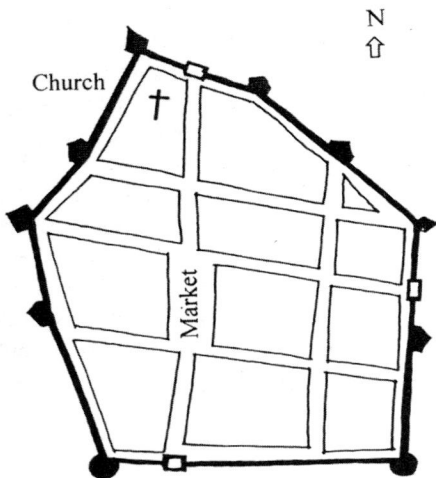

Fig.53: 1622 plan, Coleraine, County Derry.

COLERAINE

Coleraine, in County Derry, emerged through a development progression similar to that of Derry. The site was an Early Christian settlement located on the River Bann, which was taken over and promoted by the Normans. During the early Plantation period, the area passed through various hands, until it came under the control of Thomas Phillips, who had secured a market charter and a town grant by 1611. Two years later, the Irish Society acquired Phillips' interests and took over the development of the town.

As in the case of Derry, a map of 1622 offers a clear view of the walled town as it then existed (Fig.53). The map shows a layout similar to Derry, although the grid is slightly skewed, so that streets and cross streets fail to form a right angle. Internally, the map shows a rectangular market place the church in the northern corner of the town. Significantly, the town wall follows an irregular circuit and results in irregular shaped blocks, particularly at the corners. The walls themselves were built of clay, incorporated a system of four corner and five intermediate bastions as well as three town gates. These were spaced irregularly around the circuit, outside of which was a moat. Today, little survives of the structure, although the Plantation street pattern still forms the core of the town.

PORTARLINGTON

The laying-out of Portarlington, in County Laois, followed the same regular plan used in Derry, although smaller in scale. The town was founded by Lord Arlington, on a site formed by a tight bend in the River Barrow. A foundation date is not known, but the town map of about 1678 shows the town laid out so as to virtually fill the land made available by the river (Fig.54). In planning terms, the layout shows a cross-linear plan with a central market square and market house. The building plots are characteristically long and narrow. The town plan also includes a church site, located adjacent to the market area. The town defences are lightly marked on the map, and follow closely the line of the river which acts as a natural moat. The fortifications are clearly based on the Renaissance models and contain seven arrow-head angle bastions – one at each corner. The map also indicates a large rectangular bastion, on the landward side of the town, which may be related to a town gate. Today, nothing survives of the town wall, although the street layout and market square still remain.

JAMESTOWN

Jamestown was the smallest of the Plantation walled towns, and had its origins in about 1622, when Sir Charles Coote commenced to lay out his new town on the banks of the Shannon in County Leitrim. Curiously the town was positioned well back from the river bank and the nearby bridge, which must have minimised its strategic value in terms of controlling the river and its crossing. The internal arrangement of the town was elementary and consisted of a linear street plan, flanked on both side with the burgages (Fig.55). The original town charter of 1622 incorporated the walling of the town. This was achieved by enclosing the rectangular-shaped town with a stone wall. This included six bastions, one at each corner and an intermediate bastion on each of the long sides. A main gate was built at either end of the main street and this was supplemented by a small water gate which gave access to the riverbank. The town had no integral church; but it was probably intended that the remains of a friary, directly outside the northern gate, would fulfil this function. Today, only fragments of the wall survive as well as the stump of the northern gate (Fig.56).

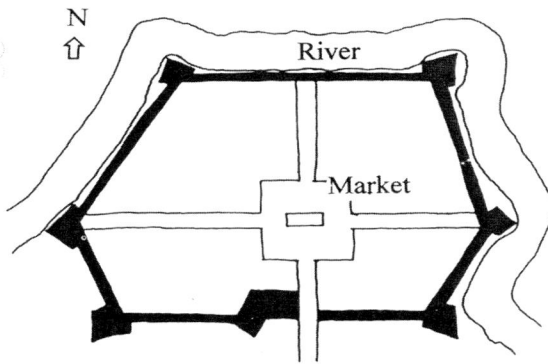

Fig.54: 1678 plan, Portarlington, County Laois.

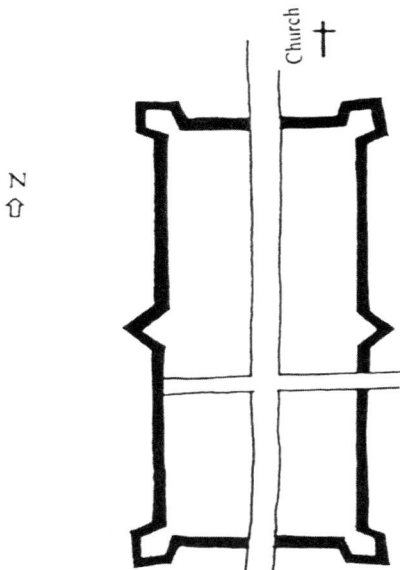

Fig.55: Jamestown, County Leitrim.

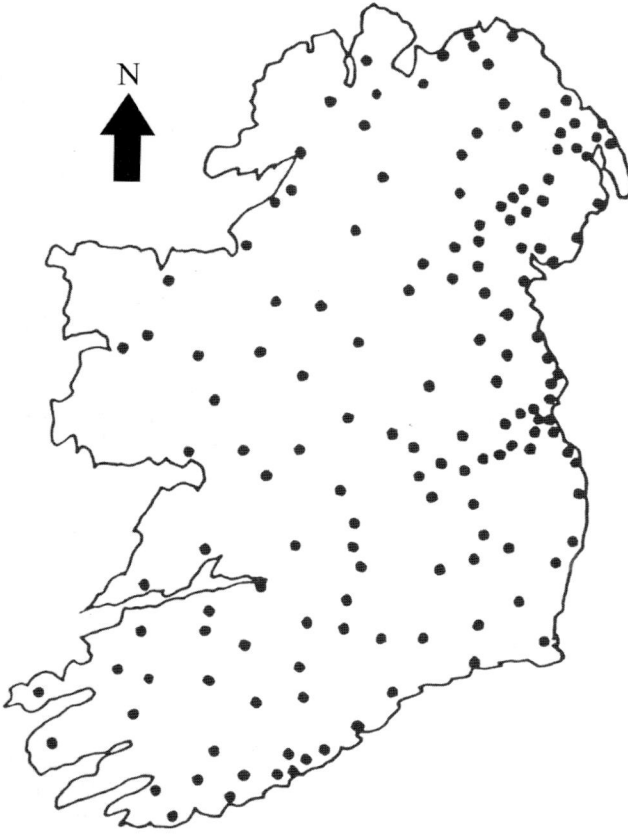

Fig. 56: 1700, Irish Town Network.

SURVIVAL

In the overall context, the Plantation towns made two contributions to the national town foundation movement. Firstly, Renaissance town-planning ideals that included geometric streets grid plans, formal public spaces, and star-shaped town walls, were all introduced. In addition, many new towns were planned, designed and built in a single movement.

Secondly, a range of new towns was established in areas where none existed. Ulster for instance, was given an extensive network of new and successful towns, where Belfast, Derry and Newry went on to evolve into nationally significant centres; although curiously, outside of Ulster, none of the Plantation towns rose to any great level in the national hierarchy. Notwithstanding, the plans of the Plantation towns proved remarkably resilient and in a number of cases, such as Derry, Coleraine, and Gorey in County Wexford, the original town cores continue to act as central places. In other cases, such as Belfast and Newry, the original street pattern survives, but subsequent eighteenth-century developments have resulted in the establishment of new town centres, forcing the original Plantation cores into secondary positions.

Most significantly, the Plantation period saw the completion of the Irish town network. Following this phase, no additions of any great consequence were made (Fig. 56). In this regard, Ireland was unique in Western Europe, in that after the close of the seventeenth century, the foundation of completely new towns was almost unknown.

SIX

GEORGIAN TOWN PLANNING – DUBLIN

1622 – 1845

THE RENAISSANCE

The fifth phase in the development of Irish towns, the Renaissance period, can be dated to between 1622 and 1845 – a time in Irish history more generally referred to as the Georgian period. Early Renaissance town-planning ideas had been introduced into Ireland during the Plantation period, with their emphasis on geometric forms and elaborate defences. By the seventeenth century, however, Renaissance town development in Europe had advanced considerably. The use of the grid, axial streets, squares, and octagon planning forms continued in use, but town defences were discarded, as they were no longer considered necessary. Overall, a more domestic approach to town planning had emerged. There was also a major shift in town fabric, as the characteristic Renaissance classical houses and cut stone public buildings made their appearance.

These fresher ideas reached Ireland in the early seventeenth century, but differed in one aspect from the European and British experiences. In Ireland, the Renaissance town-planning movement was confined almost solely to the extension and remodelling of the established towns and few totally new towns were initiated. The requirements of town and market charters had ceased, and lands required for development was held mainly by the individual landowners and developers, at both freehold and leasehold level. The results of these new approaches emerged first in Dublin, and later spread to the regional centres.

RENAISSANCE DUBLIN

In the case of Dublin, the beginnings of Renaissance town planning can be traced to 1622, when the Duke of Ormond took up his new appointment as Lord Lieutenant. Ormond had followed King Charles into exile in Paris during the Commonwealth and with the restoration of the monarchy he was appointed Lord Lieutenant of Ireland, as a reward for his loyalty. While in Paris, Ormond had become familiar with the success of Renaissance town planning, and when he moved to Dublin to take up his new post, he brought these ideals with him. Speed's map of about 1600 shows Dublin as a small rectangular walled city, positioned on the south bank of the River Liffey (Fig. 57). Behind its walls the fabric of the city consisted of a network of narrow streets The fabric is still medieval in character and consists of a range of tightly packed wooden framed and stone buildings, with Dublin Castle in the south-east corner. The map also shows the emerging suburbs on the north, south and east side of the city.

Prior to Ormond's appointment, ideas for the expansion of the city had already been considered. Sir Humphrey Jervis had secured a large tract of land on the north bank of the Liffey and he had obtained the approval of the previous Lord Lieutenant, the Earl of Essex, to build a bridge across the river and lay out a new suburb. Ormond gave his support to the Jervis proposal, but with a proviso. In the original scheme, Jervis had intended to lay out the new development with its houses backing on to the river. Ormond suggested that the houses be built so as to face the river, and that a wide, paved quay be constructed along the river edge. This ruling was highly significant for the future of Dublin, as it set the precedent for the creation of one of the city's most powerful physical features: a system of wide riverside roads and footpaths, which today stretch along both banks of the Liffey.

Ormond also involved himself in two other major civic projects, both of which were to influence the course of the city's expansion: the Phoenix Park and the Royal Hospital. Ormond was unimpressed with his quarters in Dublin Castle and he proposed creating a new Vice-regal residence. With this in mind, he enclosed a royal deer park of some 8,000 hectares on an area of land immediately to the west of the city – which ultimately evolved into the Phoenix Park. He then moved his residence from the Castle and set up the King's House at Chapelizod. At the same time, he set about building the Royal Hospital – a home for retired soldiers – on an extensive site at Kilmainham, on the south bank of the Liffey, directly opposite the new park.

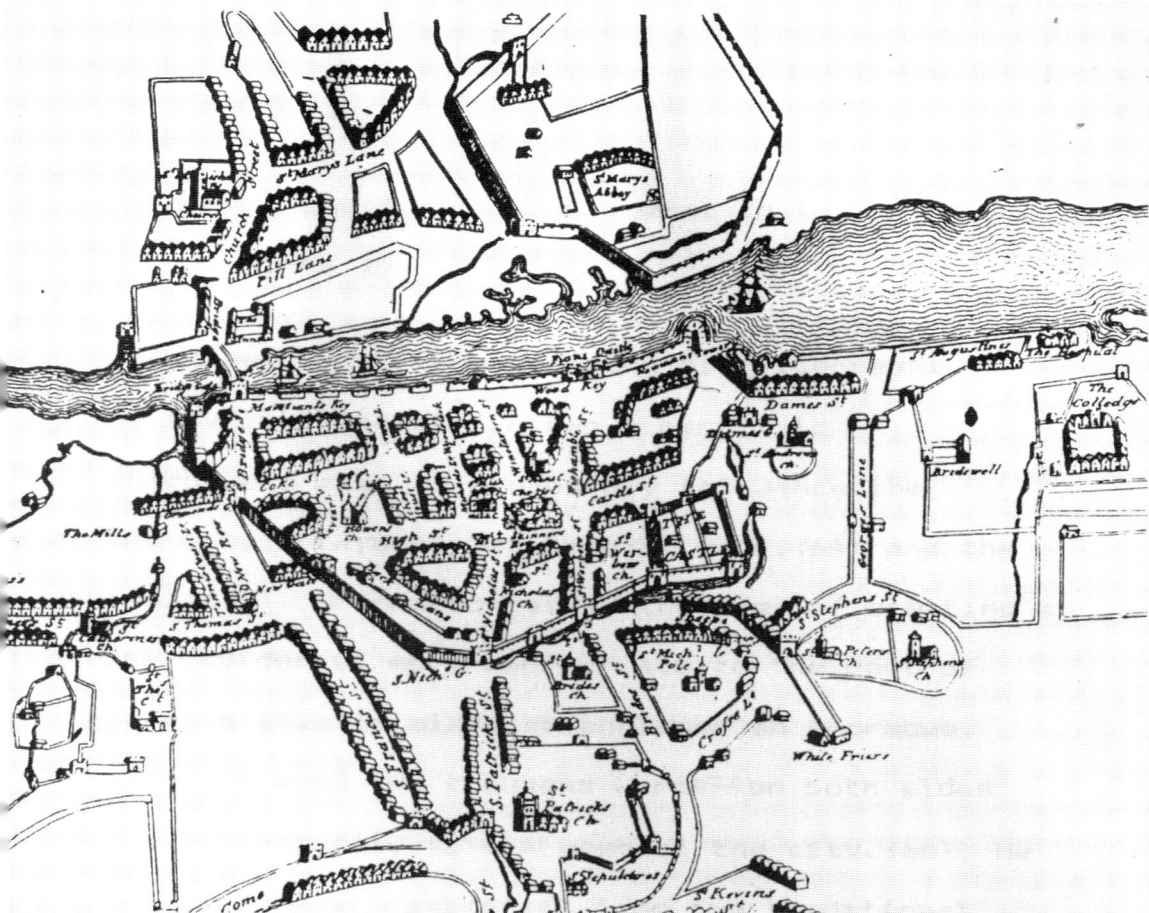

Fig. 57: Dublin, c.1600.

The consequence of the Phoenix Park and the Royal Hospital was that any westward expansion of Dublin was prevented. This, in effect, set in place a basic framework for the Renaissance city. In the centre lay the main city fabric. To the west and east lay the Phoenix Park and Dublin Bay respectively and, running like a narrow thread through the centre, the River Liffey with its new quays. Following this, Dublin then embarked on a period of hectic urban expansion. On the north side of the Liffey, the owners of the Moore Estate began to develop their lands alongside that of the Jervis Estate and on the south side of the river, the Aungier and Brabazon families began to develop their lands.

STREETS AND SQUARES

The Williamite War of the late seventeenth century caused a brief halt to Dublin's growth, following which development began again. On the north side of the city, Jervis continued to develop Capel Street and Jervis Street. To the east of him, the Earl of Drogheda began laying out Henry Street, Mary Street, and Earl Street. On the south side of the city, Sir Francis Aungier continued to develop his lands, and east of this Joshua Dawson and Viscount Molesworth began laying out Dawson Street, Nassau Street, Molesworth Street, and Kildare Street. In about 1714, a new presence, Luke Gardiner, made his appearance on the north side and began buying out the interests of both Jervis and Drogheda, so that by the middle of the century, he had emerged as the principal developer on the north side of the city – a position mirrored by the Fitzwilliam family, who operated extensively on the south-east side of the city. None of these early Renaissance developments were of themselves very extensive, neither did they form part of any overall comprehensive town plan. Nevertheless, a number of key features stand out. These include Henrietta Street and Gardiner's Mall on the north side of the city, and St Stephen's Green and Molesworth Street on the south side.

Henrietta Street was the first uniform 'Georgian' street to appear in Dublin and consisted of thirteen houses, laid out by Luke Gardiner in 1725 (Fig. 58). The term Georgian refers to the Classical-inspired Renaissance style in architecture and town planning, practiced in the British Isles during the reigns of the Georgian kings. That is, in Ireland between about 1700 and 1845. What distinguishes Henrietta Street is the fact that it was conceived as a formally-planned piece of eighteenth-century town design, comprising a single street, lined on both sides with a regular footpath and a row of similar terraced houses, all laid out to a uniform building line (Fig. 59). The houses had no front gardens; but were separated from the footpath only by a shallow railed area at basement level.

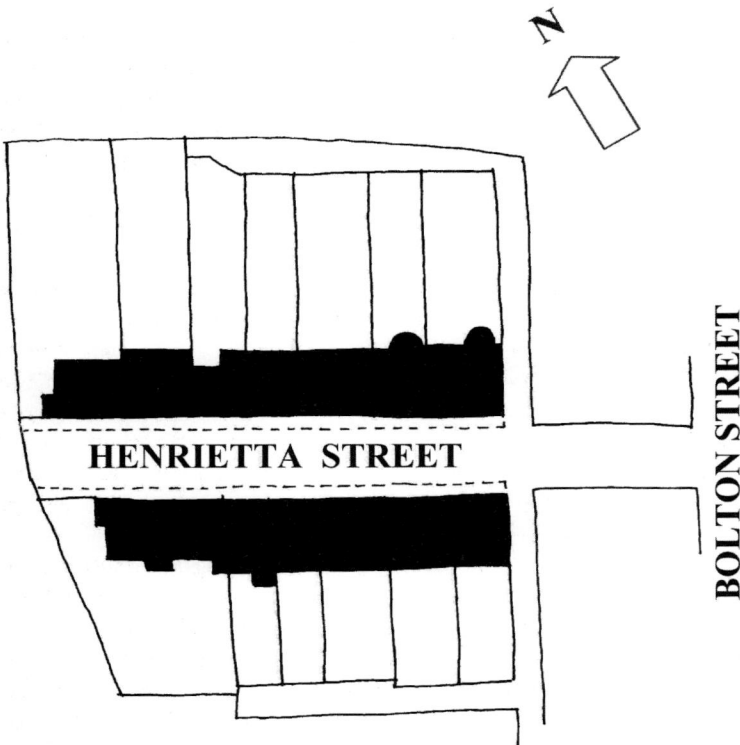

Fig. 58: Layout of Henrietta Street, Dublin.

Fig.59: Henrietta Street, Dublin.

In 1749, Gardiner embarked on a more ambitious undertaking when he laid out a magnificent new development Gardiner's Mall – the precursor of the present O'Connell Street. The mall took the form of an elongated garden square with the central lawn separated from the flanking carriageways by a system of walls, railings and obelisks – around which were arranged blocks of tall, red-brick, Georgian, terraced houses (Fig.60). In its original form, the mall started at the southern corner of Parnell Square and stretched southwards as far as the line of Abbey Street, where it ended. Only later was the line of the mall extended southwards, as far as the river, to form O'Connell Street.

St Stephen's Green was the first Georgian garden square to appear in Dublin, and it was laid out by the Corporation in 1664, on what had been an open green at the south-eastern edge of the city. The layout followed the London model and consisted of a rectangular central garden surrounded by an enclosing road – the far side of which was lined by eighty-nine building plots, which were leased off on an individual basis. These plots were used for a variety of purposes: mansions, town houses, a church, a cemetery, and a school. Curiously, no attempt was made to impose a uniform building line around the square. Nevertheless, the buildings all integrated remarkably well together and produced the largest and the most vigorous of Dublin's Georgian squares (Fig.61).

The third important feature which made its appearance in Dublin during the early eighteenth century was the 'axial' street. This consisted of a regular Georgian street which ended in an architectural feature at one end. One of the earliest uses of the axis in Dublin dates from 1720, when St Anne's Church was built in Dawson Street. The church was located at the junction of Dawson Street and St Anne Street, so as to provide a closing vista to the latter. Some time later, in 1745, the same device was used in the laying out of Leinster House in Kildare Street. Here, the architect, Richard Castles, placed the new house and its entrance gates so as to provide a dramatic closing vista to Molesworth Street (Fig.62).

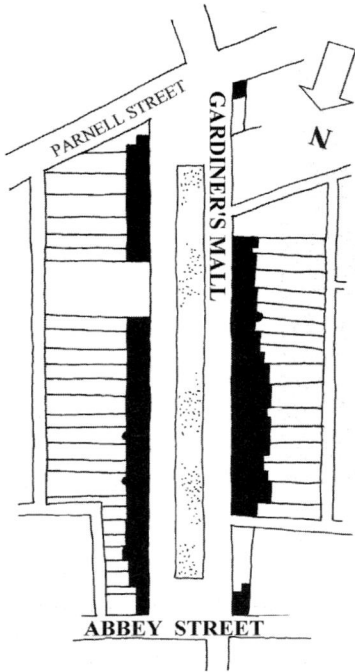

Left: Fig.60: Gardeners Mall, *c.*1750.

Below: Fig.61: St Stephen's Green, Dublin.

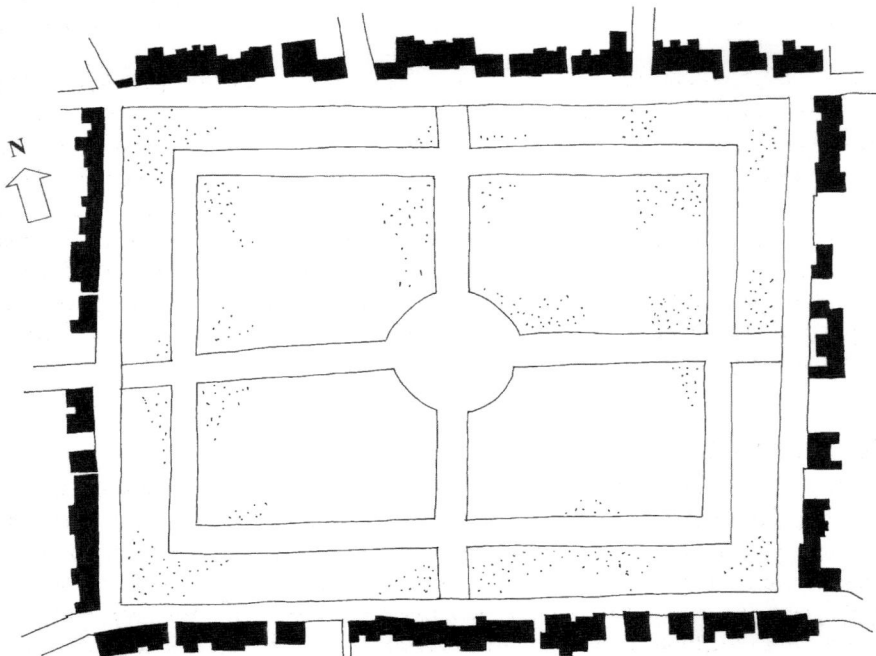

Fig.62: Molesworth Street, Dublin.

Gardiner's Mall, St Stephen's Green, and Molesworth Street made an important contribution to the development of the city, but even more significantly, they went on to have a powerful influence on the emergence of Georgian Dublin. In effect, they provided a model, where the use of the axes and closing vistas became one of the most commonly employed features in the development of the city. For example, Blackhall Place, Hume Street, North Great George's Street and Upper Mount Street all terminate in key axially arranged buildings. It should, of course, be remembered that none of these Renaissance planning elements originated in Dublin. All had their origins in Renaissance France and Italy, and all arrived in Ireland, via London, in their fully developed form.

In terms of ownership, the individual house plots of the Georgian period were held under a lease system as they were in medieval times, although the leases themselves were different. The landowner laid out the street and plot patterns of his proposed development and then leased out the house plots to a speculator or developer, who was responsible for undertaking the building work. In many instances, a major developer would take a lease on a large site and then divide up the property so that he could, in turn, lease individual house plots to smaller speculators or builders. This process was extremely beneficial to the landowner. He had little financial outlay and he received a yearly rent. In addition, the conditions of the lease ensured that all the developments conformed to his wishes. The lessee, on the other hand, risked all. He had to pay for the lease and the construction cost of the house.

GEORGIAN HOUSING

The bulk of the street architecture of Georgian Dublin consisted of standard narrow fronted Georgian houses, arranged in long uniform terraces along both sides of the streets, or around the squares (Fig.63). The houses themselves were four storeys high, over a basement and built of brick. The elevations followed a standard grid-like pattern of tall windows and brickwork, while the roof was screened from view by tall parapets. The house fronts were set back about two meters from the footpath, with a narrow sunken area between the basements and the inner line of the footpath. This provided light to the basement rooms and was enclosed by a decorated

Fig.63: Terraced town housing, Merrion Square, Dublin.

railing at ground floor level. Access to the front door of the houses was provided by a short bridge that spanned the open area. As well as the red brick houses, a number of stone-built buildings also appeared. These included individual mansions, administrative offices, hospitals, schools, clubs, and churches. All were imposing examples of Classical architecture.

THE WIDE STREET COMMISSIONERS

By the middle of the eighteenth century, the growing city had expanded more or less equally on either side of the River Liffey. Essex Bridge – the main point of access between the two sides – had evolved into the main hub of the street network. On the north side of the bridge, Capel Street was laid out on an axis to the river crossing; while on the Southside, Dublin Castle lay immediately southwards – but with a direct link between the bridge and the castle obstructed by a narrow building block. In 1757, it was decided to formalise the Capel Street/Dublin Castle axis, by cutting through the obstructing block so as to link the castle directly with the bridge. In order to achieve this, a special commission was formed with the purposes of 'making a wide and convenient Way, Street, or Passage from Essex Bridge to the Castle of Dublin'. The setting up of the Wide Streets Commission, as it came to be known, was not in itself a unique event. Other comparable bodies were being formed elsewhere in the British Isles, for similar purposes, during the same period. What was unique about the Dublin Commission was the level of power and influence it accumulated, and the breadth of its achievements. Significantly, the members of the Commission were drawn from amongst the highest levels of the community, including members of the House of Lords, the House of Commons and Dublin Corporation. Their vision for Dublin was the creation of an imperial capital.

In 1757, a plan was prepared by the Commission, showing the proposed new street, cutting through the obstructing block and terminating in a small square in front of the Castle (Fig.64). In the event, the project was only partially completed. The new street, Parliament Street, was opened in 1762, but the square was abandoned and the land ultimately became the site of the Merchants Exchange (currently the City Hall), which offered a dramatic closing vista to the new Capel Street axis.

After the opening of Parliament Street, the Commissioners continued with their meetings and discussions on the various aspects of the city development, although, in practical terms, little was achieved. Then, in 1781, an act was passed by Parliament which allowed for an extension of the Commission's interests and the funding of its operations through the levy of a coal tax. This power was further strengthened in 1790, when it was enacted that no new streets, or no continuation of an existing street, could be undertaken without the approval of the Commissioners; and again in 1792, when the authority of the commission was extended to cover an area of land extending half a mile beyond the line of the Circular Roads. The Commission had succeeded in becoming a powerful planning authority, equipped with the legal and financial ability to transform Dublin into an imperial capital.

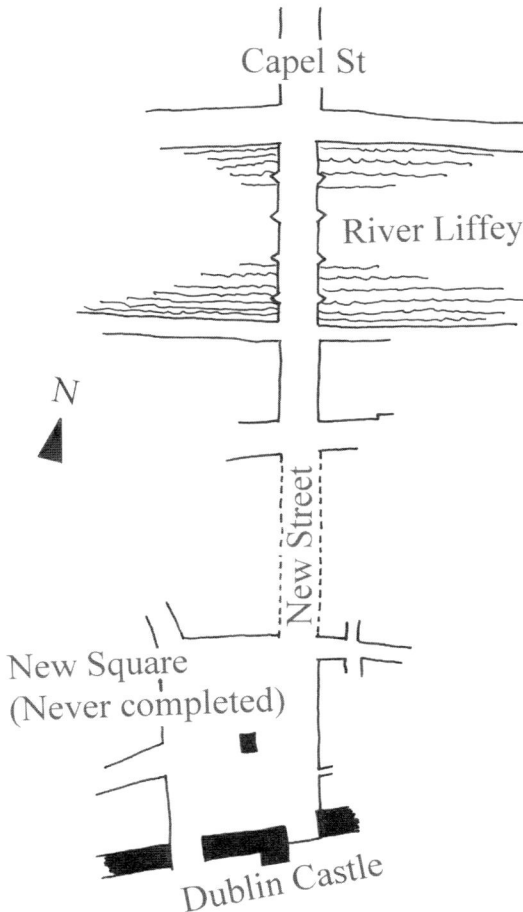

Fig.64: Parliament Street, Dublin.

In operational terms, the Commissioners imposed their ideals for the development of the city both directly, where the projects were carried out by the Commissioners themselves, and indirectly, where new developments were undertaken by developing landowners. Where the Commission was directly involved, such as in the creation of Parliament Street and Westmoreland Street, or the widening of Dame Street and Kevin Street, they were responsible for the land purchase, design, enabling work, and leasing of the properties. In the case of the private development projects, such as were undertaken by the Gardiner and Fitzwilliam estates, it was necessary that the approval of the Commission be obtained before any proposal could be undertaken. In this way, the Commissioners were able to ensure that all development proposals in the city were carried out in conformity with their wishes. The Commissioners did not, of course, plan the layout of Dublin in the strict town planning sense. The essential form of the city had already largely been established. What they achieved was the disciplining of the overall street patterns.

THE GEORGIAN CITY

In its fully developed form, Georgian Dublin was made up of three major elements: the centre core area, the surrounding street patterns, and the city perimeter. Even before the Wide Street Commission was established, the predominance of a number of the city streets had began to emerge. These included the north/south parallel lines of Capel Street and Gardiner's Mall and the east/west line of Dame Street. Although these streets were initially unconnected, they formed the basis of a formal street structure which straddled the River Liffey and upon which the Commissioners were able to build.

With the creation of Parliament Street, the first link in the establishment of the city core had been forged. The Capel/Parliament Street axis was now linked to Dame Street. In 1782, work began on the extension of the line of Gardiner's Mall (subsequently renamed O'Connell Street) southwards as far as the Liffey. At the same time, a new bridge was built across the river and in 1800 a new street, Westmoreland Street, was cut through the adjoining building fabric, to link the new bridge with Dame Street. In the process, the integrity of Gardiner's Mall was lost; but the city acquired a new geometric core which included O'Connell Street, O'Connell Bridge, Westmoreland Street, Dame Street, Parliament Street, Essex Bridge, and Capel Street (Fig.65). In addition to the street network, the axial link incorporated a remarkable range of stone-built Classical buildings: the Rotunda Hospital, Trinity College, the Houses of Parliament (now the Bank of Ireland), and the Merchants Exchange (now the City Hall) – all strategically sited on corners. All of these buildings had been built prior to the emergence of the city core, yet they were cleverly incorporated into the system so as to produce a range of closing vistas.

During the same period, the Commissioners were also engaged in the process of clearing and realigning the banks of the Liffey. They supervised the laying into position of a system of unified quays which today flank the river and stretch from the river mouth as far as the Phoenix Park – effectively completing Ormond's riverside boulevard concept. In addition, two major quay-side buildings were added to the arrangement: the Four-Courts, upriver from the Capel Street axis, and the Custom House, downriver from O'Connell Street. Later, the General Post Office was built on the east side of O'Connell Street. This was followed by the erection of Nelson's Pillar, a tall Doric column, topped with a statue of the admiral, in a central axial street position adjacent to the post office building. This has recently been replaced by a tall metal obelisk.

Outside of the central core, the Wide Streets Commissioners were equally active, as they set about the task of implementing a comprehensive street-remodelling programme, in the process of which a city-wide system of wide streets was created. Large sections of the city wall were removed, existing routes were re-aligned and widened, new streets cut through the established grain, and a suite of new squares, crescents, octagons, and axial alignments was created. In fact, most of the broad street system of present-day Dublin, including Abbey Street, Baggot Street, D'Olier Street, Gardiner Street, Kevin Street, and Mount Street, owes its existence to the efforts of the Wide Streets Commissioners.

In total, the scale of the involvement of the Wide Streets Commission on the development of Georgian Dublin was extensive and a discussion on all of their achievements and influences would be beyond the scope of this guide. However, the work of two of the cities most significant developers – the Gardiner and Fitzwilliam families – will demonstrate the range and level of accomplishments achieved by the Commissioners.

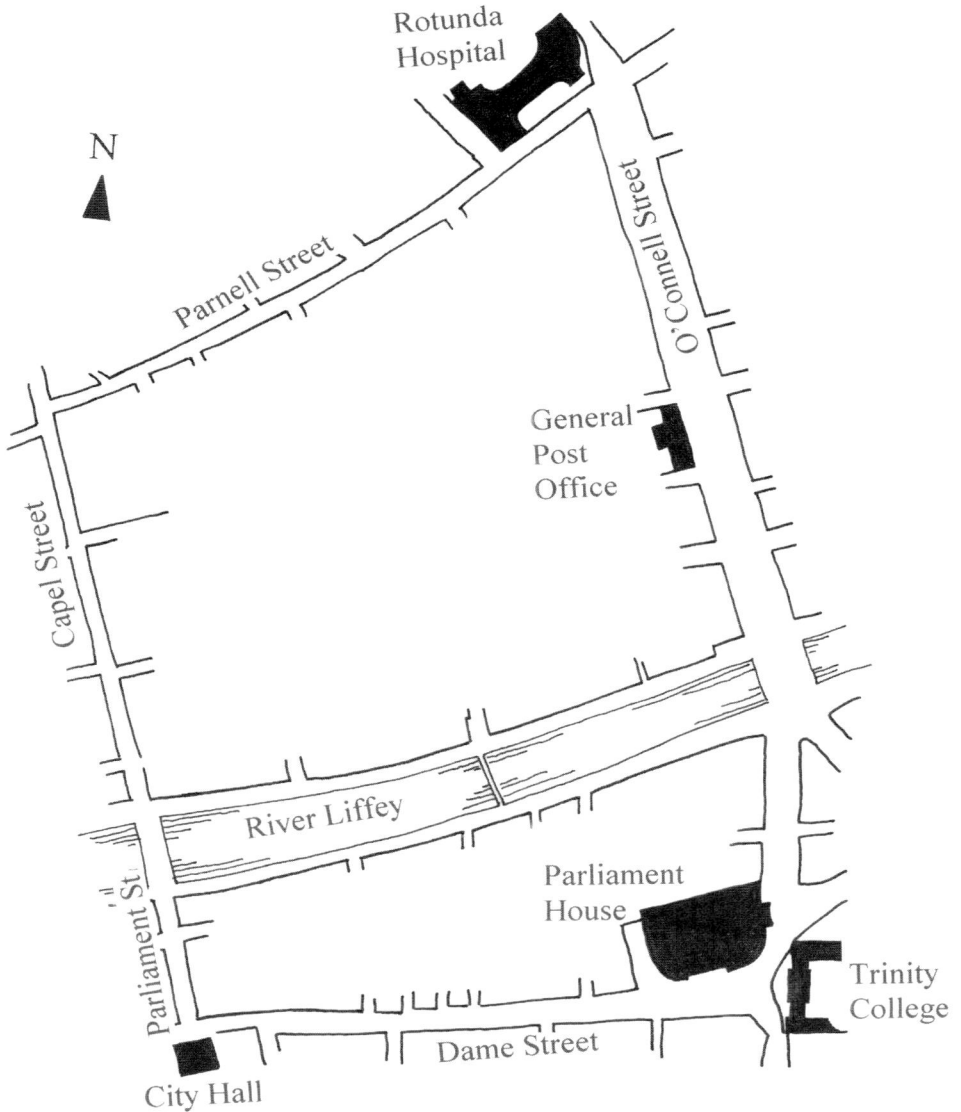

Fig.65: Central Core, Dublin.

The main thrust of the Gardiner Estate development, on the north side of the city, lay along the course of Gardiner Street which was made up of four interconnected elements: Beresford Place, Gardiner Street, Mountjoy Square, and the Royal Circus. Gardiner Street was the main spine of the complex and it was envisaged as stretching in a long north-western curve from the riverside Custom House Quay to the Royal Circus (Fig.66). When Gandon's new Custom House was completed on the north bank of the Liffey, in 1784, it formed the termination and closing vista to several merging streets: Gardiner Street, Lower Abbey Street, and Store Street. In 1795, Gandon re-organised this intersection by the introduction of a magnificent crescent of town houses, Beresford Place, which curved around the north side of his new Custom House. This was a remarkable urban concept, with the granite-white facade of the Custom House presenting its face to the river, set against the curved back-drop of tall red brick town houses. In addition, the Custom House closed the vista to each of the intersecting roads including Gardiner Street. Gardiner Street itself consisted of a broad thoroughfare flanked on both sides by a footpath and a succession of tall housing blocks, which rose in tiers with the gradual rise of the road.

Mountjoy Square was located on the east side of Gardiner Street, about half-way along its route, and was arranged so that the axis skimmed along the western edge of the square. It consisted of a square central garden, surrounded by blocks of red-brick terraced housing. It was envisaged that the Gardiner Street axis would terminate in the Royal Circus. This was to be an

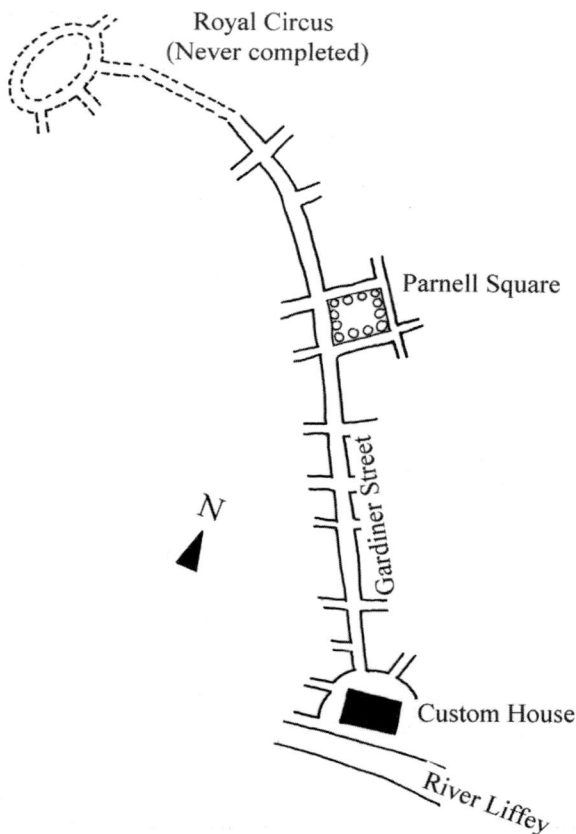

Fig.66: Gardiner Street Axis, Dublin.

oval-shaped central garden, surrounded by terraces of housing. Unfortunately, the project was never completed, although it appears on a number of eighteenth-century maps. Today, many of the Gardiner Street terraced-house blocks have been replaced and the effect of Beresford Place was shattered in the nineteenth century, when a railway viaduct was permitted to crash through the crescent, damaging both the crescent and the closing vistas.

On the south side of the city, Lord Fitzwilliam laid out two adjoining garden squares on his land: Merrion Square and Fitzwilliam Square. Merrion Square was laid out in 1762 to the design of James Ensor and is by far the largest of the six Dublin squares. The central garden was rectangular, with the eastern side taken up by the grounds of Leinster House. Fitzwilliam Square, on the other hand, is far more successful from a spatial point of view. It is more intimate in scale, perfectly square in plan, and projects a highly emphasised sense of urban enclosure.

One of the more interesting aspects of the Fitzwilliam complex is the way the squares are linked together (Fig.67). The south side of Merrion Square was laid out along an axis which stretched from the rear of Leinster House, along the square and Upper Mount Street, to terminate at St Stephen's Church in Mount Street Crescent. At the same time, an extensive cross axis was set up, which extended across the eastern side of the square, intersected the other axis, continued southwards across Baggot Street, through the eastern side of Fitzwilliam Square, and finally terminated at Leeson Street.

At the same time as the establishment of the city core area was in progress, the creation of a formal city perimeter was also being considered. In 1763, a separate commission was established to oversee the laying out of the Circular Roads. On the north side of the city, the North Circular Road was laid out on a great convex arc from the Phoenix Park in the west, to the confluence of the Tolka with the Liffey in the east. On the south side of the city, the South Circular Road

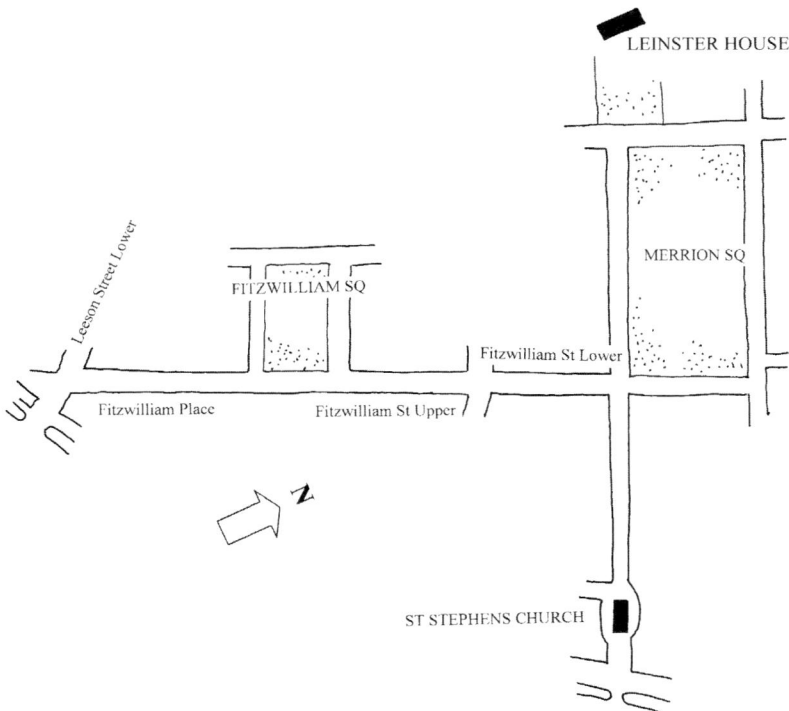

Fig.67:
Fitzwilliam
and Merrion
Square,
Dublin.

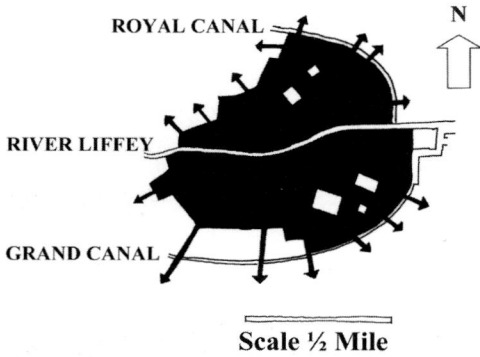

ROYAL CANAL

N

RIVER LIFFEY

GRAND CANAL

Scale ½ Mile

Fig.68: Georgian Dublin, *c*.1845.

followed a corresponding arc from Kilmainham in the west to the confluence of the Dodder with the Liffey. Although initially conceived as a matter of military expediency, to provide for a rapid deployment of troops around the city, the carrying out of the work was eventually taken over and completed by the Wide Street Commissioners. In town planning terms, the Circular Roads served as a formal oval boundary to the Georgian city and this curved perimeter was later strengthened, towards the close of the eighteenth century, by the building of two canals, the Royal Canal to the north, and the Grand Canal to the south. Each of these canals was laid out parallel to, but just outside, the line of the Circular Roads (Fig.68).

DECLINE

In 1800, the Act of Union was passed, and Ireland was absorbed into the United Kingdom. The effect on Dublin was dramatic and it rapidly shed its imperial status. The Irish Parliament no longer functioned and large numbers of the politicians and aristocrats moved away, either to London, or to their country estates in the provinces. As a consequence, the Dublin housing market declined and, after the first quarter of the century, fewer and fewer development projects were undertaken. Even before the Union, the residential pattern of the city had begun to change. The building of the Custom House on the north bank of the river made the north side of the city less desirable, and the fashionable quarter shifted south of the river, to the Merrion-Fitzwilliam Square area. The entire north-side area entered a period of deterioration and after the Union it degenerated into tenements.

On the south side, the effects of the Union were less catastrophic. There, the houses of the vanished aristocracy were taken over by the middle and professional classes, who lacked the finances and interest in the continuing development of the city. Development did not, however, cease entirely. The Wide Street Commissioners continued with their improvements, although on a much reduced scale. Westmoreland Street, D'Olier Street and Fitzwilliam Square were completed and in about 1830 the last of the Dublin Georgian squares, Mount Pleasant Square, was laid out.

By this time, after a growth period of nearly a century and a half, the development of Georgian Dublin was complete. During that time, its status had moved through an administrative circle – from a colonial outpost, to an imperial capital, and finally back into provincial obscurity. Nevertheless, the city could boast an extensive Georgian legacy: the Liffey-side boulevards, six garden squares, some smaller public open spaces, and a body of outstanding public and domestic Georgian architecture.

SEVEN

GEORGIAN TOWNS

1700 – 1845

GEORGIAN DEVELOPMENT

Outside of Dublin, the scope of Georgian town development was equally strong, as across the country, the square, the mall, and the linear axis were all employed with a level of skill and imagination that, in places, exceeded the successes of the capital. The pace was, however, slower than in Dublin and it was not until the second half of the eighteenth century that any noticeable level of development emerged, as towns and cities began to expand. Town walls were removed and extensive rebuilding and remodelling projects were undertaken everywhere. Streets were widened and straightened out, regular building lines were established, new squares and malls were often inserted. At the same time, the medieval and Plantation fabric of the towns was replaced with new Georgian houses and classical public buildings. In many cases such as Dungarvan in County Cork, Newry in County Down, Birr in County Offaly, and Limerick City, developments were extensive indeed, although completely new towns were a rarity.

FABRIC

The architecture of the larger examples, such as Limerick, closely followed the Dublin example and consisted of standard tall, red-brick, Georgian houses, arranged in uniform terraces, with consistent building lines and parapet levels. In the smaller centres, such as Mitchelstown in County Cork and Westport in County Mayo, the housing was more modest. The characteristic tall Georgian windows and vertical emphases of the houses were retained, as was uniform terracing and the long narrow building sites. However, the houses were, for the most part, two and three storeys, and significantly, the brick elevations were replaced with rendered stone walling. The parapet was also eliminated with the result that the slated roofs could be clearly seen from the streets. As was the case in Dublin, stone-built public buildings were inserted into the streetscapes, although these were more modest in scale than those of the capital. All of these changes combined to produce a regional eighteenth-century street architecture that was uniquely Irish.

GEORGIAN LIMERICK

The use of the gridiron street plan was popular in a number of regional centres and it was successfully used in Bagnalstown, Belfast, Mitchelstown, and Newtownards. However, it was in Limerick, that the landowner, Edmond Sexton Pery, exploited the grid system to its best advantage, when he began to develop his new suburb of Newtown Pery, from 1769 onwards.

The gridiron layout, used by Pery, was probably the work of the Sardinian architect Davis Ducart, with the possible assistance of a local architect Christopher Colles, who prepared a drawing of the layout, in 1769. The Colles plan shows Newtown Pery laid out on a gridiron pattern, immediately to the south of the older medieval city, and consisting of five longitudinal streets running parallel to the River Shannon, intersected at right angles by eight cross streets (Fig.69). The plan also incorporated three features into the mesh of the grid. These included two small octagons, a garden square and a system of quays that acknowledged the riverside setting of the new development.

In its execution, the building of the town followed the Colles master plan, with only minor variations. The octagons were never built, and the grid was never completed in the south-eastern corner. It was not until the late eighteenth century that any significant changes were made, when several new features were introduced. These included the repositioning of the square, the establishment of a major cross axis, aligned on the centre of the square, and the creation of a new crescent at the southern end of the longitudinal axis (Fig.70). In addition, a second small square

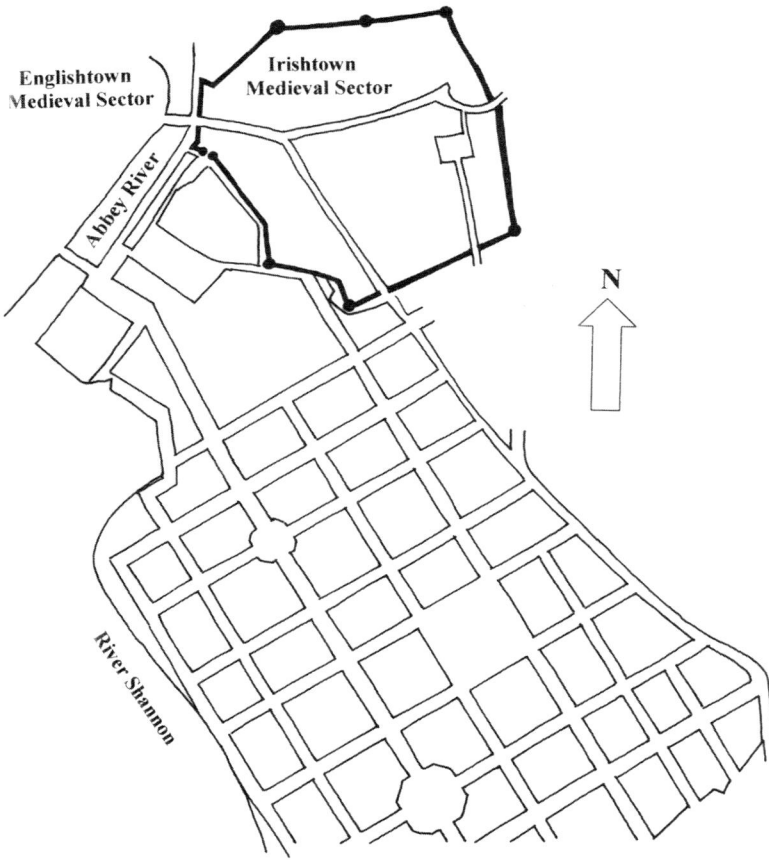

Fig.69: Plan of
Georgian Limerick,
County Limerick.

was incorporated into the complex, and a new bridge across the Shannon created a second cross axis near the northern end. Although Pery Square and its central garden were originally laid out, the overall development was never completed. Only one building block was built (Fig.71) and eventually the central garden and the surrounding section of the grid were incorporated into a municipal park in 1874. Despite this, Newtown Pery, with its gridiron master plan, its squares, crescent, axial elements, and standard Georgian housing ranks as one of the most successful and comprehensive examples of Irish eighteenth-century town planning.

MITCHELSTOWN

In Mitchelstown, the Earl of Kingston also used a grid when he laid out his new town, although on a much reduced scale to that used by Pery in Limerick. In 1776, Lord Kingston began building himself a new house to the west of the town, and shortly afterwards he commenced work on the re-modelling of the town itself. The layout consisted essentially of two parallel streets, George Street and Cork Street, which were linked together by six cross streets, all conforming to the grid pattern. Into this pattern, a garden and a market square were inserted: King's Square in the north-western corner and the Market Square in the opposite diagonal corner (Fig.72).

Left: Fig.70: The Crescent, Limerick, County Limerick.

Below: Fig.71: Pery Square, Limerick, County Limerick.

King's Square is the most notable spatial feature of the town, and it acts as the pivotal point for the setting out of the grid. In centre of the west side was the main gateway to Lord Kingston's new house and, directly across the square, Baldwin Street was laid out on an axis to the gates. In the centre of the north side was a small chapel, from where the line of George's Street was set out. The result was a pair of axial streets which intersect at mid-point in the square. In addition, George's Street was provided with a southern closing vista in the form of St George's Church of Ireland church. On the opposite diagonal of the grid, the setting out of the Market Square also incorporated an axial device. The Market House was positioned in the centre of the east side of the square, while directly opposite King Street is laid out on an axis which is closed on the western end by a single house. A distinctive feature of the King Street axis is that it operates on an upper and lower level. On the lower level, the axis stretches from King Street across the square to terminate at the Market House, while on the upper level the line carries across the roof-line of the market building to terminate at St Fanahan's Roman Catholic church located on higher ground to the east.

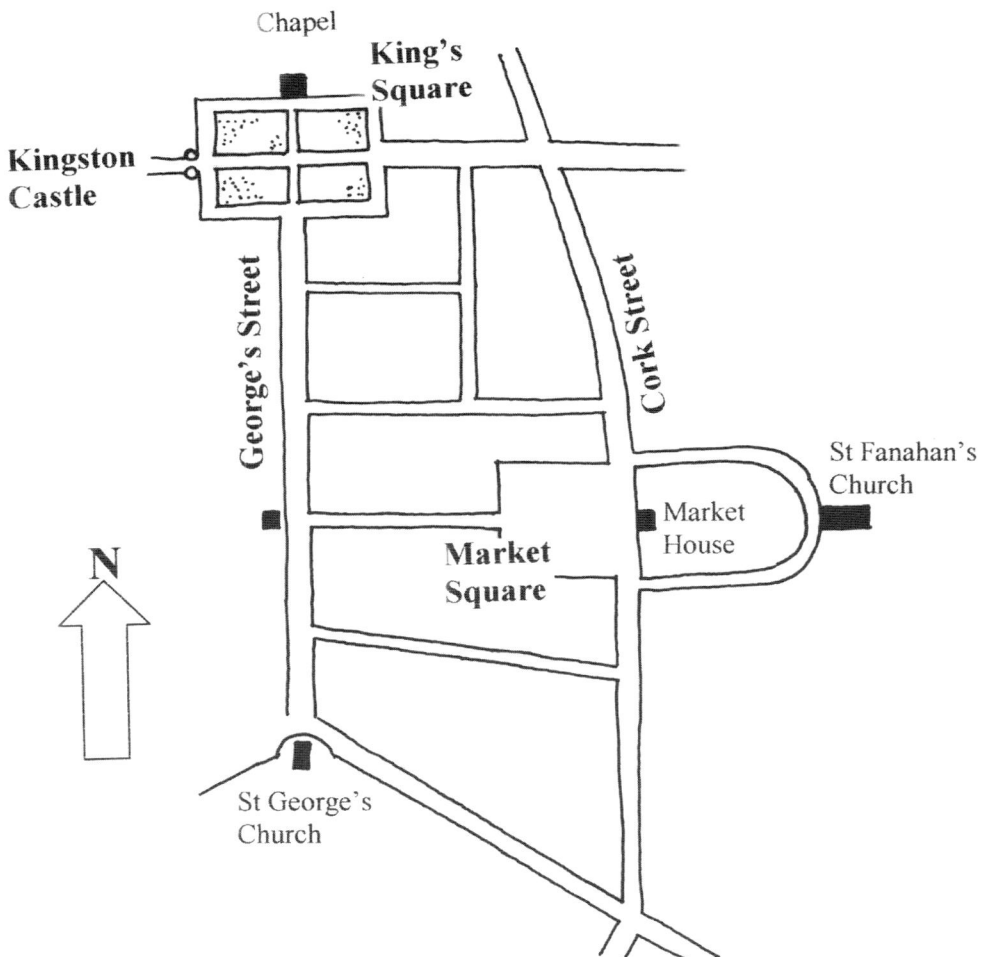

Fig.72: Layout, Mitchelstown, County Cork.

Above: Fig.73: King's Square, Mitchelstown, County Cork.

Left: Fig.74: Plan of Fermoy, County Cork.

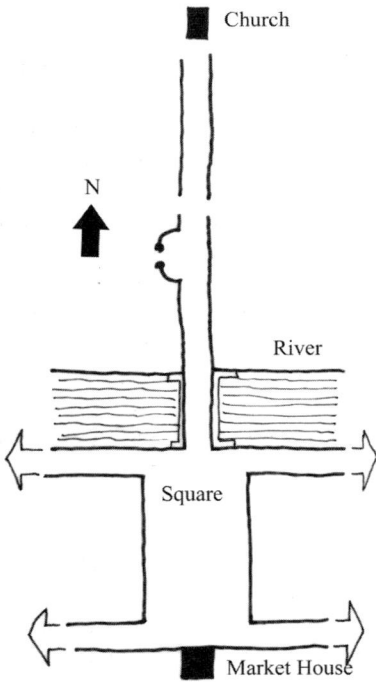

The Mitchelstown plan is very inventive indeed. King's Square for example is a delight. The central area is grassed, and the south side consists of a range of two-storey Georgian houses (Fig.73). The north side, in contrast, consists of a unique architectural complex of stone-built almshouses. The overall result is a fascinating combination, part traditional garden square and part college quadrangle.

FERMOY

In the nearby town of Fermoy, the landowner John Anderson limited the scope of his development to an axis and square, when he remodelled his town in 1791 (Fig.74). Anderson's plan took the form of a long axial street. The line of the axis began at the Church of Ireland Christ Church and followed the downward slope of the street, across the town bridge and into the town square. On the way, the line was skilfully directed between a series of architectural elements, before it terminated at the market house on the south side of the square. After leaving the church, the line of the axis was emphasised by the crescent-shaped entrance to Anderson's estate, the parapets of the bridge, and the channelling effect of the rectangular market place with its tall enclosing houses, the entire ensemble a dramatic exercise in axial planning.

NEWRY

At the beginning of the eighteenth century, Newry consisted of a Plantation town that lay on the south bank of the River Newry in County Down, although a little distance back from the river bank. In 1730, it was decided to link Newry with the inland Lough Neagh by means of a canal, in order to assist with the opening up of the hinterland around the lake. The works also involved the narrowing and channelling of the Newry River and this had the effect of creating an area of reclaimed land between the Plantation town and the river. This new land presented the opportunity for expanding the town and it was enthusiastically seized.

A map of the town prepared by John Rocque in 1760 shows how the proposal was to be laid out (Fig.75). A long main street follows the gentle curve in the river and five cross streets linked the old town, the new development and the river edge together. The most original feature of the plan was the arrangement of the axial main street. Instead of the more common practice of constructing a long street and central square, such as at Mitchelstown and Fermoy, the new street pattern of Newry consisted of three small squares spaced out along the curved line of the new street. These were positioned at the junction of three of the cross streets. The effect of this was to create an interrelated sequence of open spaces and axial planning that responded to the curved nature of the site. Unfortunately, the development was not completed as planned. The southern square was rearranged so as to slot between the new street and the old town in the form of a mall, and although attractive in itself, the amendment reduced the force of the original proposal. Today the two squares, Marcus Square and Margaret Square (Fig.76) and the axial Hill Street, still reflect the original spatial atmosphere. In addition, a number of the original tall Georgian terrace houses also survive.

BIRR

The town of Birr in County Offaly was a medieval foundation which underwent extensive additions and remodelling during the eighteenth and nineteenth centuries. These consisted of a bold axial street, a central square and two spectacular malls. In its earliest form, Birr consisted of an Early Christian settlement positioned on the south bank of the Camcor River. During the Norman period, a castle was built on the far bank of the river. This was followed by the laying out of a new town, that consisted of a rectangular market place, linked to the castle by a single street.

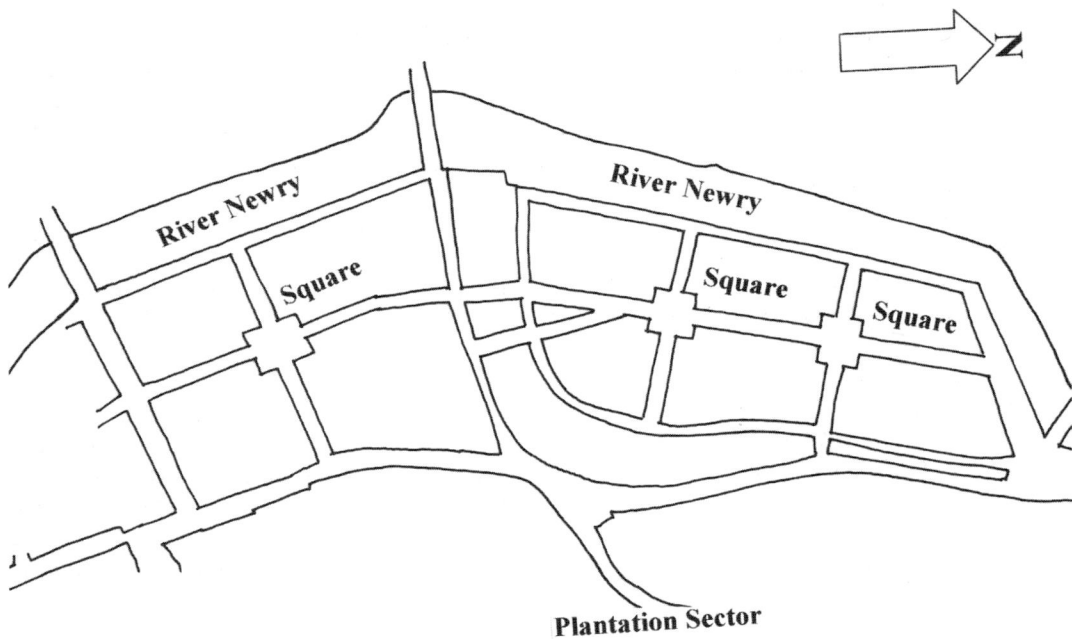

Fig.75: Plan of Newry, County Down.

Fig.76: Margaret Square, Newry, County Down.

The eighteenth-century development of the town took place in a series of stages. First a long axial street, Main Street, was laid out from the town bridge. This intersected the edge of the market place on its northerly course. Half way along the new street a new market square, Cumberland Square, was laid out. This had a tall central obelisk that emphasised the line of the axis. Following this, two malls were created: John's Place on the east side of Cumberland Square and Oxmanstown Mall in the west side of the Main Street axis (Fig.77).

John's Place has an extended triangular form with entrances at each of the corner points – the most western of which opens directly off Cumberland Square. Internally the arrangement consists of a triangular green surrounded by a carriageway and a range of terraced houses. The houses were unusual for the period in that they were given front gardens (Fig.78). Near the centre of the green, a statue marks a cross axis with St John's Hall on the north side of the mall. Oxmantown Mall is an altogether more formal exercise in street geometry, and consists of an axial roadway, closed at either end by a bold architectural feature: the entrance gates to Birr Castle estate on the east and St Brendan's Church of Ireland church on the west. Both the castle gates and the church were built in a Gothic Revival style. The street itself consisted of a central carriage way, with a tree-lined lawn and a narrow service road on the south side. On the far side of the road, a range of terraced houses were built, and these were again provided with front gardens (Fig.79). The architecture of both malls is outstanding: a rich collection of terraced town houses and individual Palladian-inspired villas.

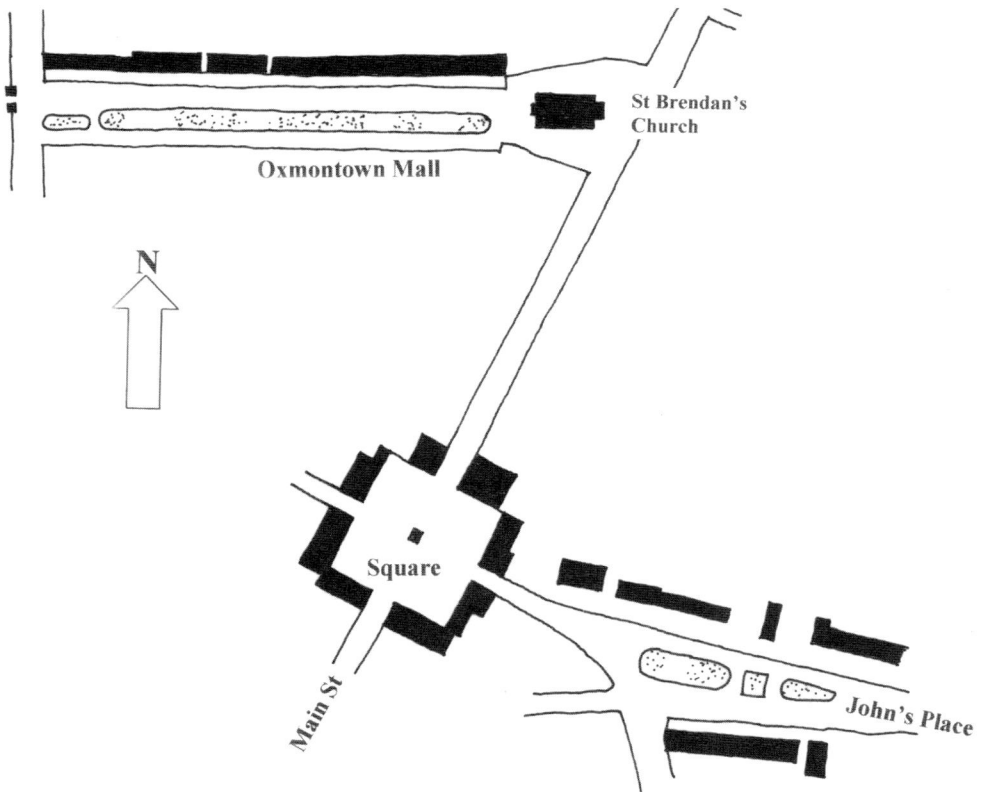

Fig.77: Plan of Birr, County Offaly.

Fig.78: John's Place, Birr County Offaly.

Fig.79: Oxmantown Mall, Birr, County Offaly.

NEW TOWNS

Completely new towns were rare in Georgian Ireland and the few that were established, such as Castlewellan in County Down, were small in scale and remained so. The one exception to this was Westport, which went on to increase in size and importance by stages. Castlewellan was laid out and developed in two stages: Old Town and New Town (Fig.80). In about 1760, Lord Annesley laid out his original town in the form of a half-octagonal market place, around which the modest Georgian terraced houses of the period were arranged. The entrance gates to the Annesley estate opened directly of the market place and a market house was built in a curiously off-centre position. An interesting feature of this stage of the town development is the extensive back lanes that were provided to serve the backs of the house plots. Some time later, it was decided to extend the town and a second market space was laid out on the west side of the Old Town. The plan here, however, differed from the original market place in that it was given two straight ends and two curved sides, into which the houses were set in a crescent-like arrangement. The new market place was provided with its own market house, again in an off-centre position, but the service lanes were extended only to the houses on the eastern end.

WESTPORT

The layout of Westport offers an excellent example of the use of multiple planning elements including an octagon, a mall, a fair green, and a range of axial alignments. The town had its origins in the early eighteenth century, when the Earl of Altamont put into effect a series of improvements to his house and estate at the edge of Clew Bay in County Mayo. One aspect of this involved the creation of an extensive park within the estate lands. As the village of Cathair na Mart lay in the way of the park-land proposal, Altamont decided that the village should be moved. He therefore offered the villagers the choice of two possible relocation sites: Westport Quay, or the site of the present town. The villagers choose the latter, and some time about 1750 work started on the new town, which was completed in a series of stages. In the first of these stages, the new town was laid out on an irregular cross-roads plan centred on the intersection of High Street, Shop Street, Bridge Street, and Mill Street.

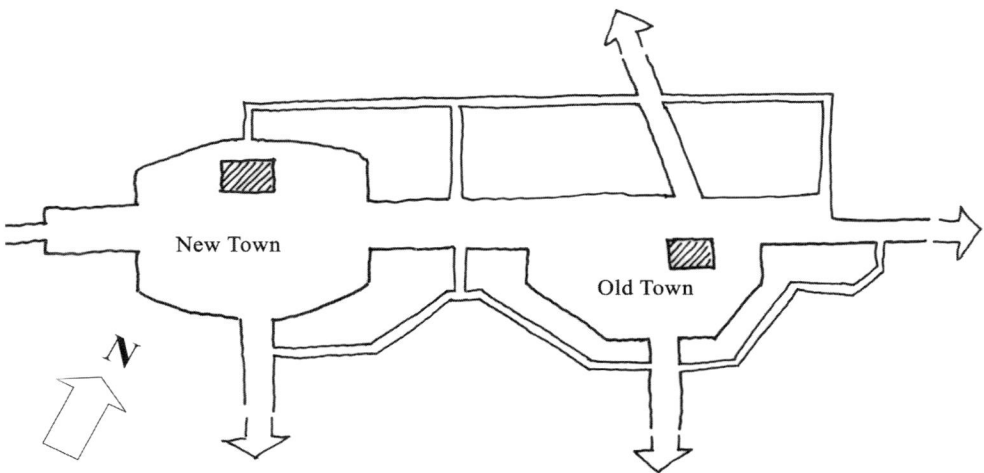

Fig.80: Plan, Castlewellan, County Down.

In 1793, the Third Earl, who was created the Marquis of Sligo, decided to extend the town. Using the initial crossroads as a base, Lord Sligo added a series of elements to the northern and western edge of the village. These included the long Peter Street/James's Street axis, an Octagon, a Mall, and a Fair Green. In effect, the loose cross-roads system was transformed into a formal geometric pattern. By 1820, the Marquis' scheme was to all intents complete, and a map prepared in that year by Henry Browne shows the principal elements of the town all in place.

Today, Georgian Westport offers a view of a highly formalised approach to urban planning (Fig.81). The Octagon presents a range of terraced houses, with the market house positioned at mid-point, so as to close the vista from Shop Street (Fig.82). In the centre of the Octagon, a tall, slim Doric column acts as a central point on the line of James Street, and at the same time provides a closing vista to Shop Street. This acts as a visual connection between the initial stage of the town and the later additions.

In laying out the Mall, on the north-west side of the town, Lord Sligo succeeded in creating what is, unquestionably, one of the most accomplished examples of mall planning in the country. He re-routed the course of the small Carrowbeg River and channelled it into a formal canal. This was flanked on either bank with a tree-lined boulevard. The canal bank was emphasised by a low stone wall, in addition to which the watercourse was crossed by two triple-arched bridges (Fig.83). Both sides of the Mall are lined with a range of eighteenth- and nineteenth-century buildings: the Inn, the Methodist Chapel, the Gothic-Revival Roman Catholic church, and a range of terraced houses

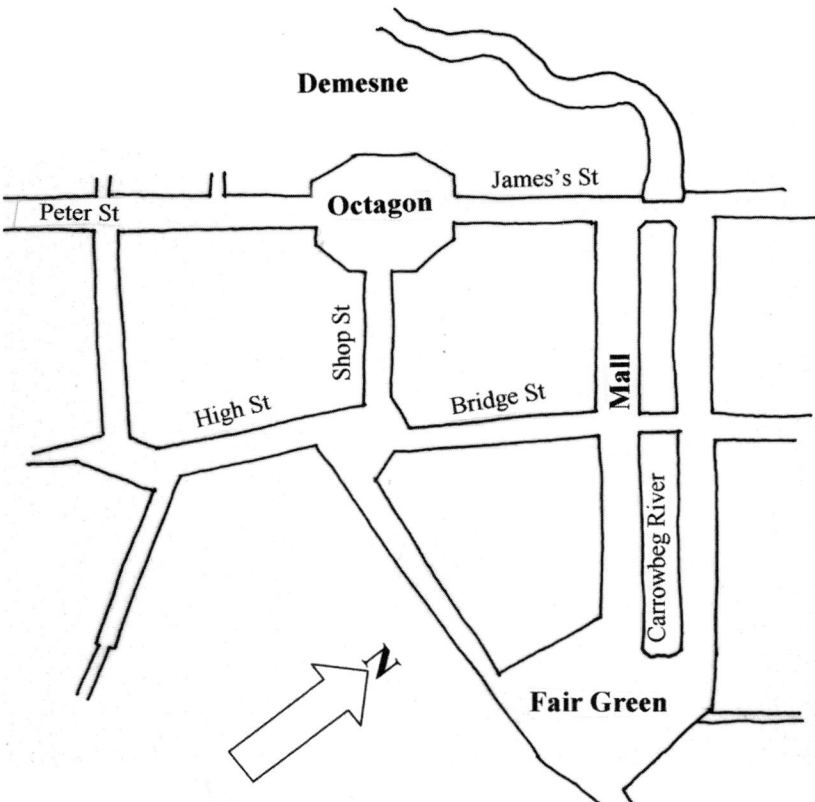

Fig.81: Plan, Westport, County Mayo.

90

Fig.82: The Octagon, Westport, County Mayo.

Fig.83: The Mall, Westport, County Mayo.

The Fair Green lies at the eastern end of the Mall and consists of a triangular green where the Mall, Mill Street and Altamont Street converge. It is enclosed by a series of two-storey eighteenth-century houses. Anywhere else in Ireland the Fair Green would stand out as a notable feature, but in Westport it is inclined to be visually overshadowed by the nearby Mall and the Octagon. Although the layout of Westport is frequently held up as one of the most notable examples of Georgian town planning in Ireland, this is not strictly the case. Westport did not start with a formal master plan, but had a plan skilfully superimposed on it. This process of coupling the various planning elements into a dynamic whole is where the real significance of Westport lies.

DECLINE

Outside of Dublin, the impact of the Act of Union was a great deal less and, if anything, an impetus was added to regional town development process during the early years of the nineteenth century, particularly in the western areas of the country, where towns like Belmullet, Clifden, and Roundwood were established. The pace of growth was not, however, sustained for very long, and was brought to a halt by the Famine in 1845. After the Famine, the country suffered a dramatic reduction in population. The towns were deprived of growth and development, and most entered into a period of stagnation. Large scale development ceased throughout the country, and the Georgian town-planning movement in Ireland was brought to a close.

In an overall context, Georgian Dublin, with its wide streets, squares, and network of Georgian terraced housing, ranks as one of the foremost Georgian cities of the British Isles. Elsewhere, developments were more modest in terms of scale. Nevertheless, when considered together, the collective body of Irish eighteenth-century town development represents an outstanding example of achievement, where the street planning, the open spaces, and the architecture act together to offer an experience that is eminently successful. This was the golden age of Irish town planning and development, which, in so many instances, achieved a level of success never since equalled. In contrast, the Victorian development that followed was a much more modest and restrained affair.

EIGHT

VICTORIAN EXPANSION
1845 – 1914

VICTORIAN EXPANSION

The Victorian period is the sixth and final phase in the historic development of Irish towns being considered in this guide. This phase began after the 1845 Famine and consisted mainly of laying out suburban extensions, where lands were available particularly around the edges of the established centres. In these new suburban areas, enterprising landowners laid out new streets and spaces and leased off plots to builders and developers, much as they had done in Georgian times, although in a much reduced scale. In most cases, the Georgian planning elements such as the grid, the square, and the axial layout, continued to be used. Formal landscape elements were incorporated into most development projects, however. In addition to the suburbs, changes also took place in the town cores, which acquired more and more retail and administrative facilities as the period developed. Coupled with this, the Victorian period saw the introduction of a whole new range of civic, religious, and administrative buildings, in order to satisfy the increasing complexity of Victorian life.

In terms of the new Victorian fabric, the uniform eighteenth-century Georgian street architecture gave way to the more complex Victorian buildings with their mixture of antique styles, varying building heights, and differing shapes and colours. These range from small brick-fronted Georgian-like houses, to mock Gothic and Romanesque churches (Fig.84) and public buildings, along with buildings in other historic styles, such as Tudor and Jacobean (Fig.85). Above all, decoration is the hall mark of Victorian architecture, coupled with the use of multiple colours and surface finishes, often in a single structure. In addition to the new buildings, a large number of Georgian town houses changed from residential to retail use. The upper floor of the houses remained in residential use, but the ground floor was converted into shopping. This was achieved by creating a wide opening at ground level and facing it with a decorated shop-front, that consisted of wooden uprights spanned with a high level sign-board or fascia (Fig.86). The overall effect, particularly where a number of adjoining premises were altered in this way, was to dim the character of the original Georgian streetscape.

VICTORIAN DUBLIN

As was the case in earlier phases, Victorian developments first emerged in Dublin. Here, despite the loss of its parliamentary status after the 1800 Act of Union, the city continued its outward expansion. During this process, it still retained its administrative and commercial significance, but gradually the wealthy business- and middle-class citizens moved to the new suburbs, which were in the process of being created outside the lines of the canals, particularly on the south side. Most of Georgian Dublin, particularly on the north side, was thus left to the poor and it began to descend into slums. On the south side, the areas around Merrion and Fitzwilliam Squares became largely the domain of professional families, and occasional pockets of new housing were built to cater for clerical and skilled workers, particularly along the eastern ends of the North and South Circular Roads.

The Georgian street-scape of the city also experienced changes, as commercial and retailing units began to make their appearance in some of the major streets, such as O'Connell Street, Dame Street and Grafton Street. Most of these centre city changes, however, had little effect on the overall Georgian form of the capital. The one exception was the arrival of the railway. The first rail service was introduced between Dún Laoghaire and Dublin in 1834. This was followed by a series of other services which converged on the city from the various regional centres. This resulted in the building of a string of railway stations around the edge of the Georgian sector, with only one route, the north-south line, crossing the Liffey and cutting its way through the city fabric.

Left: Fig.84: Gothic Revival Church, St Stephen's Green, Dublin.

Below: Fig.85: Tudor revival style house, Ranelagh, Dublin.

Fig.86: Georgian house with Victorian shop-front inserted, Westport, County Mayo.

THE VICTORIAN TOWNSHIPS

The great impact of Victorian development in Dublin was, however, felt beyond the lines of the Grand and Royal canals, where a number of new, independent townships were established to house the wealthy sections of the community who had deserted the city centre. By 1880 there were eleven such townships. These included Clontarf and Drumcondra on the north side of the city, and Pembroke, Rathmines, Kilmainham, Blackrock, Kingstown (Dún Laoghaire), Dalkey, Killiney, and Bray on the much more extensively developed south side (Fig.87).

Although the various townships lacked a formal town plan, each was made up of a network of individual residential projects, often arranged around a central administration and retail zone. The latter very often consisting of a single shopping street. In Rathmines, for instance, the southern end of Rathmines Road contained the main administrative and shopping sector of the township, particularly around the intersection of the axis with Belgrave and Rathgar roads. Here, the Town Hall, the library, the fire station, two churches, three religious houses, a number of schools, and a series of retail shops were concentrated together along both side of the street, while at the edge of these new commercial zones the shopping gradually gave way to the standard blocks of terraced housing.

In planning terms, the layout of the various residential developments within the townships followed the earlier Georgian principles, with wide roads and squares lined with residential terrace blocks. A typical example of this was the Fitzwilliam development in Pembroke, which was laid out in the late eighteen hundreds. This consisted of Waterloo Road, Wellington Road and Clyde Road, arranged in a basic grid within a triangular site, with links to the previously established lines of Baggot Street and Leeson Street Upper (Fig.88). These developments followed the eighteenth century patterns, with blocks of tall, narrow-fronted terraced houses, long narrow rear gardens, and a system of narrow mews lanes at the rear of the plots.

The house blocks, however, incorporated three new features. Initially, there was little difference between the elevations of the Victorian blocks and those of the earlier Georgian period, except the introduction of light elements of decoration, particularly on the street facades. More significantly, the building lines of the house blocks were stepped well back from the line of the footpaths, so as to provide each house with an individual front garden. Thirdly, the new roads were given a landscape treatment that included of a line of trees along the outer edges of the footpaths – in effect establishing a network of landscaped boulevards (Fig.89). Initially, the terrace blocks were exceedingly long and it was only in the eastern sector, around Clyde Road, that short blocks and individual houses made their appearance.

The Fitzwilliam development in Pembroke was one of the first in Ireland to herald the changes in architectural style and to introduce the use of formal urban landscape ideals. Following this, the extensive use of landscape and decoration became standard features of Victorian developments – elsewhere in the townships, and later in other Irish cities and towns.

A typical example of the developed Victorian style can be found around Belgrave Square in Rathmines. This includes a garden square, a long axial boulevard, and a public park. Work on the square began in around 1850 and followed the earlier Georgian format of a central garden framed by an enclosing carriageway, which was itself lined with blocks of tall, brick fronted, terraced housing. The one difference was that the houses were given front gardens (Fig.91). From the south corner of the square, Belgrave Avenue extends southwards in a gentle curve as far as the junction with Belgrave Road and from here Palmerston Road continues southwards again in a gentle curve, as far as Palmerston Park (Fig.92).

As well as incorporating a curve, the Palmerston carriageway was flanked on both sides with trees, which introduced a formal landscape element into the streetscape. This landscape treatment was strengthened by additional tree-planting in the generous front gardens of both terraced and detached houses. At the southern end of Palmerston Road, Palmerston Park was laid out between 1881 and 1893 as a semicircular public park, on lands provided by the developer, Lord Palmerston. Although the line of the axes carries through the park in the form of a pedestrian walkway, the roadway divides and follows the semicircular outline of the park, to join up again on the south side. Thus, the park act as a termination to Palmerston Road, and at the same time, offers a continuation of the axial line. On the south side of the park, the axis continues along Orchard Road to terminate at St Philip's church, which is positioned on the far side of Temple Road (Fig.90).

The houses immediately surrounding Palmerston Park were amongst the last to be completed and they clearly express the characteristic features of High Victorian architecture and planning. On the north side of the park, the long terraced blocks have been replaced by shorter blocks, while on the south side, the development consists of a series of large individualistic houses, set in individual landscaped plots, many bearing romantic names, such as 'Richview', 'The Orchards' and 'The Chalet.

Not all Victorian developments were laid out in as monumental a form as the Fitzwilliam and the Palmerston Road axis. Most examples of Victorian urban development consisted of two-storey housing and only in exceptional cases were roadside treescapes provided. The front garden, however, remained a consistent feature of the Victorian era, if on occasions it was reduced to a token gesture. For example, a network of simple geometric streets, such as Temple Gardens and Beechwood Avenue, was laid out and developed on either side of Palmerston Road axis (Fig.93). These streets were more modest than the Palmerston Road development and consisted of small-scale housing blocks which incorporated a range of minor elevational features, such as coloured brickwork and decorative windows. These roadways lacked formal tree planting, but the Victorian landscape effect was emphasised by the inclusion of private front gardens.

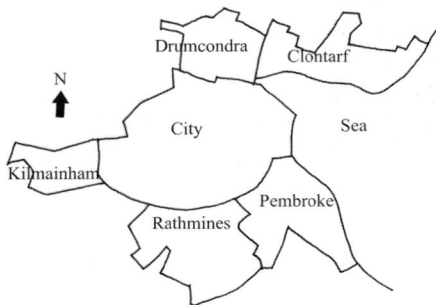

Left: Fig.87: Victorian Townships, County Dublin.

Below: Fig.88: Plan of Fitzwilliam Development, Dublin.

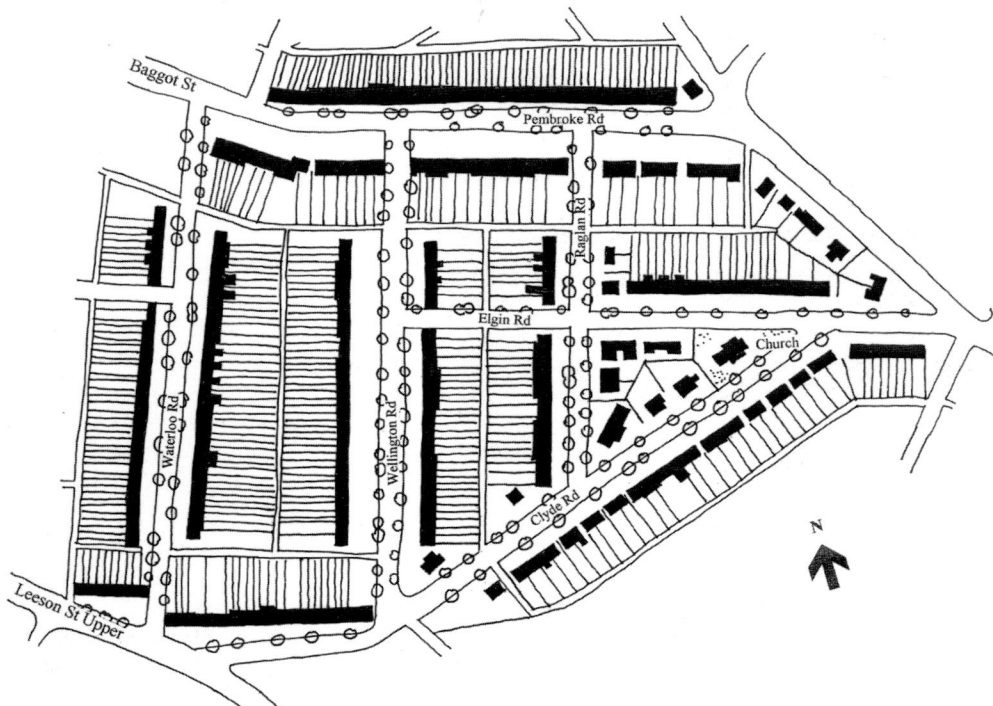

Fig.89: Wellington Road, Dublin.

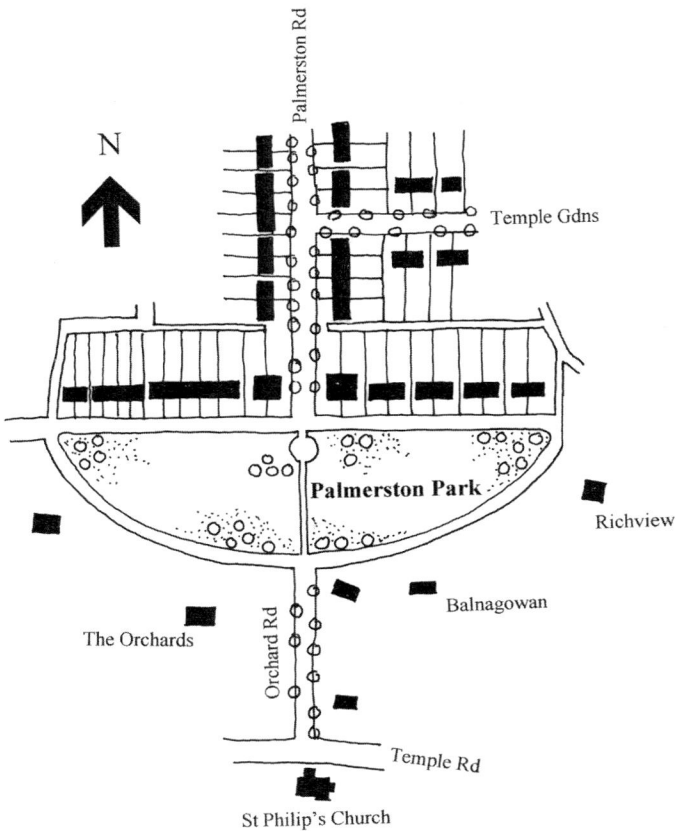

Fig.90: Plan of Belgrave Square/Palmerston Road Axis, Dublin.

Fig.91: Belgrave Square, Dublin.

Above: Fig.92: Palmerston Road, Dublin.

Opposite: Fig.93: Beechwood Avenue, Dublin.

ARTISAN HOUSING

Although the great bulk of nineteenth-century development in the townships was focussed on the requirements of the wealthy, a number of small artisan-type developments were also completed. These were undertaken with the specific goal of providing housing for the less well off sectors of the community and included, for example, the Dublin Artisans' Dwelling Company housing at Stoneybatter and Harold's Cross, as well as the Iveagh Trust apartment development at Christchurch. Although they conformed, in spirit, to the current Victorian planning ideals, these developments were laid out so as to achieve as high density of housing as possible, by the elimination of gardens and their replacement with tiny backyards.

Stella Gardens in Irishtown and the Meath Street development in the Liberties offer two interesting approaches to the laying out of artisan housing. Stella Gardens was laid out on a tight gridiron plan which was located between Irishtown Road and the River Dodder, with an open green stretching between the houses and the riverbank (Fig.94). Apart from the green, no other landscape features were incorporated into the project, although a number of the houses were provided with miniature front gardens. However, the severity of the grid was reduced by the scale of the streetscape and by the grouping of the houses into individual blocks of single- and double-storey terraces, each block decorated in cottage-style architecture (Fig.95).

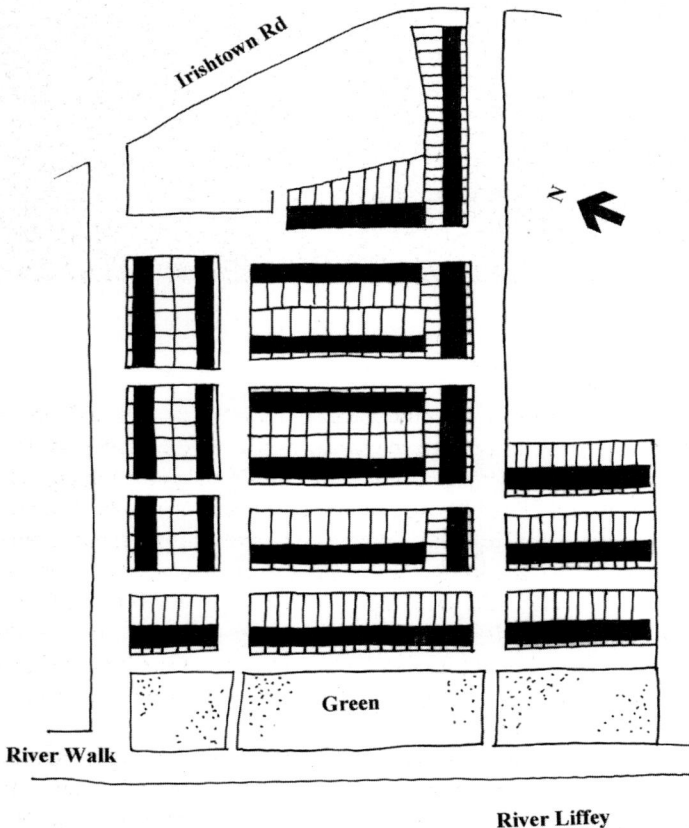

Fig.94: Plan of Stella Gardens, Dublin.

Fig.95: Cottages, Stella Gardens, Dublin.

The Dublin Artisans' Dwellings Company development, off Meath Street, was laid out in around 1882, to a plan which was altogether more sophisticated than that used in Stella Gardens. This development consisted of four small squares, set into in a four-block grid (Fig.96). The squares were formed by laying out a range of plain single-storey cottages in a pinwheel fashion (Fig.97), with a further range of brick double- and single-storey cottages arranged around the outer perimeter of the grid (Fig.98). In addition, a continuous narrow service lane was positioned between the backs of the cottages. Landscaping was kept to an absolute minimum and consisted of four small house gardens positioned around the octagon at the centre of the complex. Over the years, a number of small but accumulative changes have distorted the original layout in parts. Thus, the layout presented in Figure 96, must be seen as indicative of the original morphology, around the time of its completion.

In contrast to the Stella Gardens and the Meath Street projects, the artisan housing around the Stoneybatter area on Dublin's north side was much simpler in terms of layout and architecture. Here a large complex of streets was laid out to basic grid plan (Fig.99), that incorporated a range of plain double- and single-storey cottages, with no front gardens and a small yard at the rear (Fig.100).

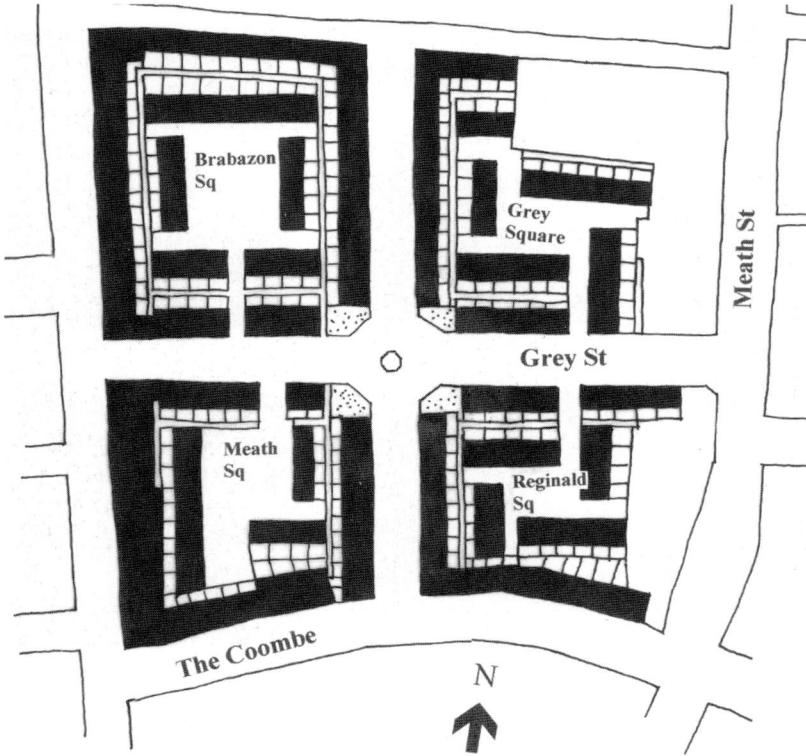

Brabazon
Sq

Grey
Square

Meath St

Grey St

Meath
Sq

Reginald
Sq

The Coombe

N

Left: Fig.96: Plan
of Meath Street
Development,
Dublin.

Below: Fig.97:
Single-storey
cottages, Meath
Street, Dublin.

Above: Fig.98: Double–storey cottages, Meath Street, Dublin.

Below: Fig.99: Stoneybatter, Dublin.

Fig. 100: Double-storey cottage, Stoneybatter, Dublin.

VICTORIAN BELFAST

Despite the scale of the Victorian developments in Dublin, it was Belfast that was most affected by Victorian town developments. The initial settlement here consisted of a small Plantation town laid out by Sir John Chichester in 1604, at a point where the River Farset joined the River Lagan. Some eighty years later, the town was well developed and was enclosed by a defensive wall, with a range of short and corner bastions. The little River Farset flowed through the centre of the town, dividing it into two sectors. The northern sector was largely built up and followed an irregular street pattern. South of the river, Belfast Castle filled the south-western quadrant with some housing built along the river front (Fig. 101).

By 1757, the castle and the town walls were demolished, the Farset had been culverted over to form High Street, and the town had begun to extend outwards. This development progressed slowly, but by 1815 an extensive gridiron pattern of largely undeveloped roads had been laid out on the north and south side of the initial settlement. At this stage, the development of the southern sector was the most advanced. Here, Donegall Place was laid out, perpendicular to High Street, and stretched southwards as far as Donegall Square. The rectangular square acted as the hub of the grid plan, that included a range of Georgian streets, which in turn supported a range of tall red-brick Georgian houses. This phase also saw the construction of the White Linen Hall in the centre of Donegall Square, as well as the development of the series of river-side quays along the banks of the Lagan.

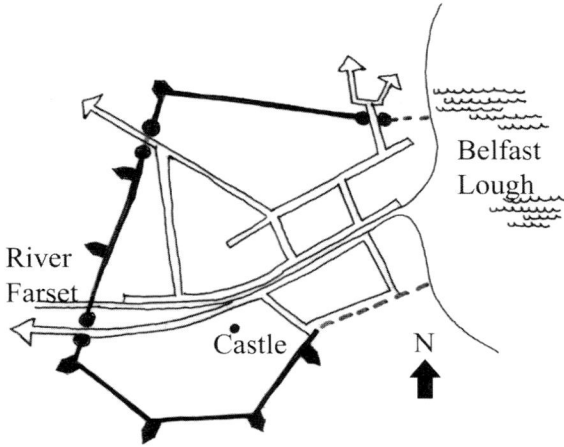

Fig. 101: Layout, Plantation Belfast, County Antrim.

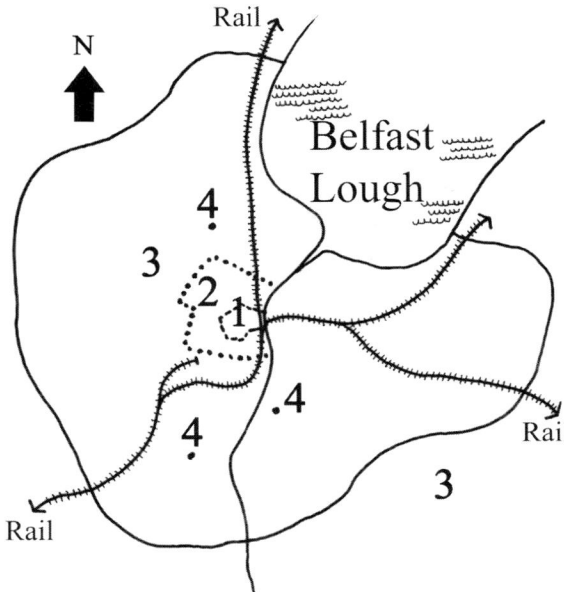

Fig. 102: Expansion of Belfast, County Antrim. (1: Plantation. 2: Georgian. 3: Victorian. 4: Public Park.)

It was, however, the infilling of these grids that initiated the dramatic emergence of Victorian Belfast (Fig. 102). This expansion phase began about the middle of the nineteenth century, and was prompted by the success of the city's industrial expansion, particularly linen manufacturing. The gridiron street networks provided a spatial framework which was gradually filled with the city's expanding Victorian fabric. At the same time, industrial zones and harbour works, along the banks of the Lagan, also developed and expanded dramatically

Like Dublin, the Victorian development of central Belfast took the form of extensive redevelopments of shopping and commercial interests, along the established street lines, particularly around the Donegall Place and Royal Avenue area. Here, new shopping and administrative centres were provided, and the city's central business sector began to emerge. In Donegall Square, the Linen Hall was replaced by the City Hall in 1896. The new structure was built in dramatic Classical Revival style and acted as a powerful focus to the Royal Avenue/Donegall Place axis.

In the new Victorian suburbs, a number of landscaped boulevards, much like Dublin's Palmerston Park, were created, particularly around the Lisburn and Antrim Road areas, where substantial Victorian houses were built on individual plots (Fig. 103). In addition, the Great Northern Railway was threaded through the city fabric from about 1840 onwards. The rail yards and terminus were built close to the site of the new City Hall, while the rail line continued across the city to service the ever expanding industrial and ship building sectors, on both sides of the Lagan. The landscaping of Victorian Belfast was limited. The extensive Ormeau Park was laid out along the east bank of the Lagan and two smaller public parks were also provided. Alexander Park was established near the Reservoir on the north side of the city, while on the south side, Dunville Park was laid out as part of an administrative hub that included The Royal Victorian Hospital, the mental hospital and St Paul's church.

It was, however, the industrial and residential development of the north and south grids, and well beyond, that provided the most extensive and significant aspect of Victorian Belfast. Here, and on the east side of the River Lagan, vast numbers of high density, artisan and industrial workers' cottages were built to house the city's workforce. The great bulk of these developments were completed without the benefit of landscaping or any form of public amenity areas. In most instances, the only open spaces provided were the tiny backyards of the houses. In the overall, the dullness of the grid and the similarity of the housing were relieved only by the presence of the occasional Victorian church or industrial building complex.

A full review of Belfast's entire Victorian housing is outside the scope of this guide, due to the vastness of its extent. However, Chadwick Street and Windsor Road, off Lisburn Road, highlight the character and uniformity of the city's typical industrial neighbourhood (Fig. 104). Chadwick Street is lined on both sides with a continuous terrace of narrow-fronted houses, packed tightly together and opening directly onto the footpaths. These houses are characteristically double storeyed, with brick fronts, and slated pitched roofs, each with a nominal back yard (Fig. 105). On one side of the street the houses were given half-round bay windows at ground level, while the corresponding houses across the street were given slightly projecting rectangular bay windows. The housing on Windsor Road is slightly different. The houses on the north side are similar to those in Chadwick Street, while those on the opposite side of the road have tiny front gardens, enclosed by low brick-built boundary walls (Fig. 106). All of the houses have a rear access through a system of narrow service lanes that run between the back of the houses block. In contrast, the houses on nearby Great Northern Street are similar in layout, but much more basic in appearance. These open directly off the footpath with neither bay windows nor front gardens (Fig. 109).

In the overall context of Belfast, it is worth remembering that the Chadwick Street and Windsor Road developments are only a tiny sample within the overall spread of city's extensive housing pattern, and it is only when viewed in this light that the full scale of Victorian Belfast housing can

Fig.103: Adelaide Park, Belfast, Country Antrim.

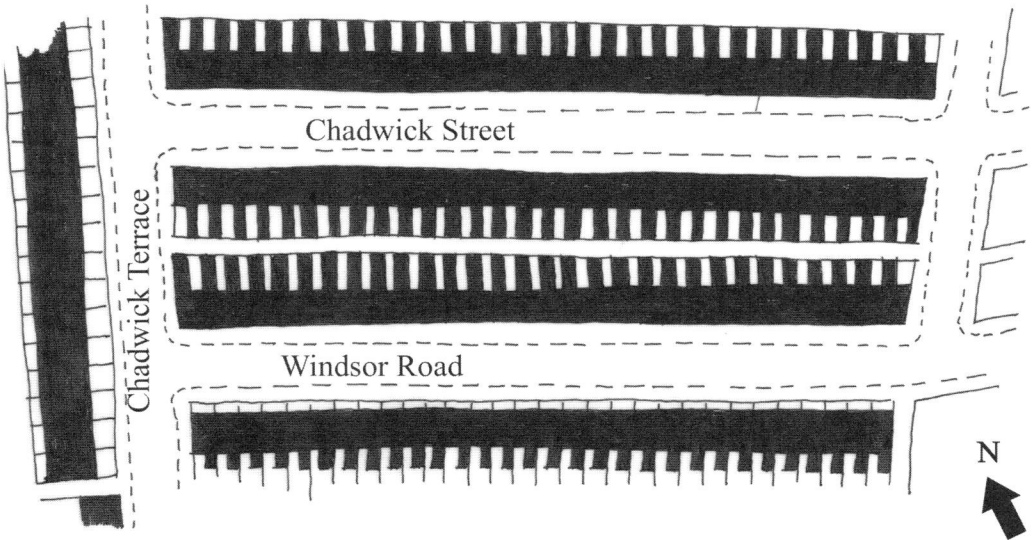

Chadwick Street

Chadwick Terrace

Windsor Road

N

Fig.104: Layout, Chadwick Street/Windsor Road, Belfast, County Antrim.

Fig.105: Chadwick Street, Belfast, County Antrim.

Fig.106: Windsor Road, Belfast, County Antrim.

Fig.107: Terraced housing, Chadwick Terrace, Belfast, Country Antrim.

be appreciated. Today, much of the original harshness of the nineteenth-century workers' housing has been softened through upgrading, new developments and environmental improvements, although some sectors survive intact, a visual testimony to the city's Victorian industrial power.

REGIONAL CENTRES

Other than Belfast and Dublin, the scale of Irish Victorian urban development was modest, and consisted for the most part of street by street extensions. Often, where development took place it concentrated, not so much on housing, but on the provision of state, local authority and religious administrative nodes, or on the laying out of small residential suburbs at the edges of established centres. In Waterford, for example, the radiating lines of the earlier medieval and Georgian city were extended westwards and southwards in a fan-like fashion, with the Victorian architecture filling the blocks between the radiating roads. Landscaping seemed to play only a minor part in the development of Victorian Waterford, except for one notable example: the Court House grounds and the People's Park, which were incorporated onto the bend of the St John's River. This new sector was laid out in the early nineteenth century, at the southern end of Catherine Street, where the new Classical-style court house was built on a dramatic landscaped site, with the sweep of the river acting as a southern boundary. The People's Park was laid out on the far bank of the river in 1857, and the two sites were linked by a visual cross axis. This began at the portico of the Court House, stretched across the front lawn of the site, crossed the river by a narrow bridge and terminated at the Bandstand, which was positioned at the central point of the park.

On the south side of the river, the perimeter of the park was marked by a system of wide roadways with a curious mix of uses. On the east side, New Street consisted of a range of industrial sites which stretched between the road and the estuary of the River Suir and included a ship yard, a foundry and a saw mill. On the western side of the park, Hardy's Road and Water Street were lined by terraced housing, the Turkish Baths and the Model School, while the open landscape of the De La Salle College lay on the south side of Park Road.

In Cavan town in County Cavan, Victorian expansion took a more formal approach in the shape of Farnham Street, which was laid out almost parallel to the town's earlier Main Street in the nineteenth century (Fig.108). By 1900, this street was complete and lined with a range of civil and religious buildings: the Roman Catholic cathedral, three churches, three community halls, the Court House, the Town Hall, a bank, a school and the gaol. In addition, the street contained clusters of terraced houses as well as a number of substantial houses on individual plots. In all of these, landscape elements played a significant part, in addition to which, a splendid public park was laid out about half-way along the street.

The growth of civil and ecclesiastical administrative centres, often in clusters such as in Cavan, was a common feature of Victorian development. This was particularly so in the case of the Catholic institutions, which tended to cluster together and often included a wide range of religious buildings, including churches, convents, monasteries and schools. These clusters, in effect, represented the expansion of Catholic influence following the Catholic Emancipation Act of 1829.

In the city of Limerick no fewer than three major clusters were established in Victorian times. These included two separate Catholic clusters, as well as a civic administrative one. On the South Circular Road a group of Catholic institutions were clustered together, immediately to the south of the city's extensive Georgian sector. The initial development of this area began as a typical early Victorian residential development, of large individual sites and houses. Following Catholic Emancipation, a number of religious bodies acquired the family homes and established a range of church-based institutions. This included five religious houses and six schools, while only a short distance away the parish church of St Joseph, another religious house and two further schools were built.

On the north bank of the River Shannon a second cluster of religious houses, schools and churches was established close to the Bishop's Palace on the North Circular Road. The two clusters lay across the river from one another, where they acted as a major focus of post-Emancipation Catholic development. During the same period, a new civic administration cluster was also laid out at the opposite side of the city. This consisted of a long and wide linear street, Mulgrave Street, which was flanked on either side by a sequence of public buildings. These included the Military Barracks, the County Jail, the Mental Hospital, a general hospital, a cemetery and a market area.

SEASIDE TOWNS

Another notable feature of Victorian Ireland was the emergence of a number of small sea-side towns around the coastline. The development of these towns was prompted by two interconnected movements: the popularisation of sea-side holidays and the introduction of train travel. As early as the end of the eighteenth century, a number of coastal villages had begun to attract visitors, particularly for the sea bathing facilities they offered. The coming of the railways in the second half of the nineteenth century boosted the concepts of seaside trips and holidays, both as a social and as a medicinal experience. This, in turn, prompted the development of a string of seaside towns around the coastline, which sought to cater for the needs of the Victorian

RC Cathedral

N

Hall

Church

Church St

Court House

Farnham St

Hall

Park

Church & Residence

Church & Residence

Town Hall

Main St

School

River

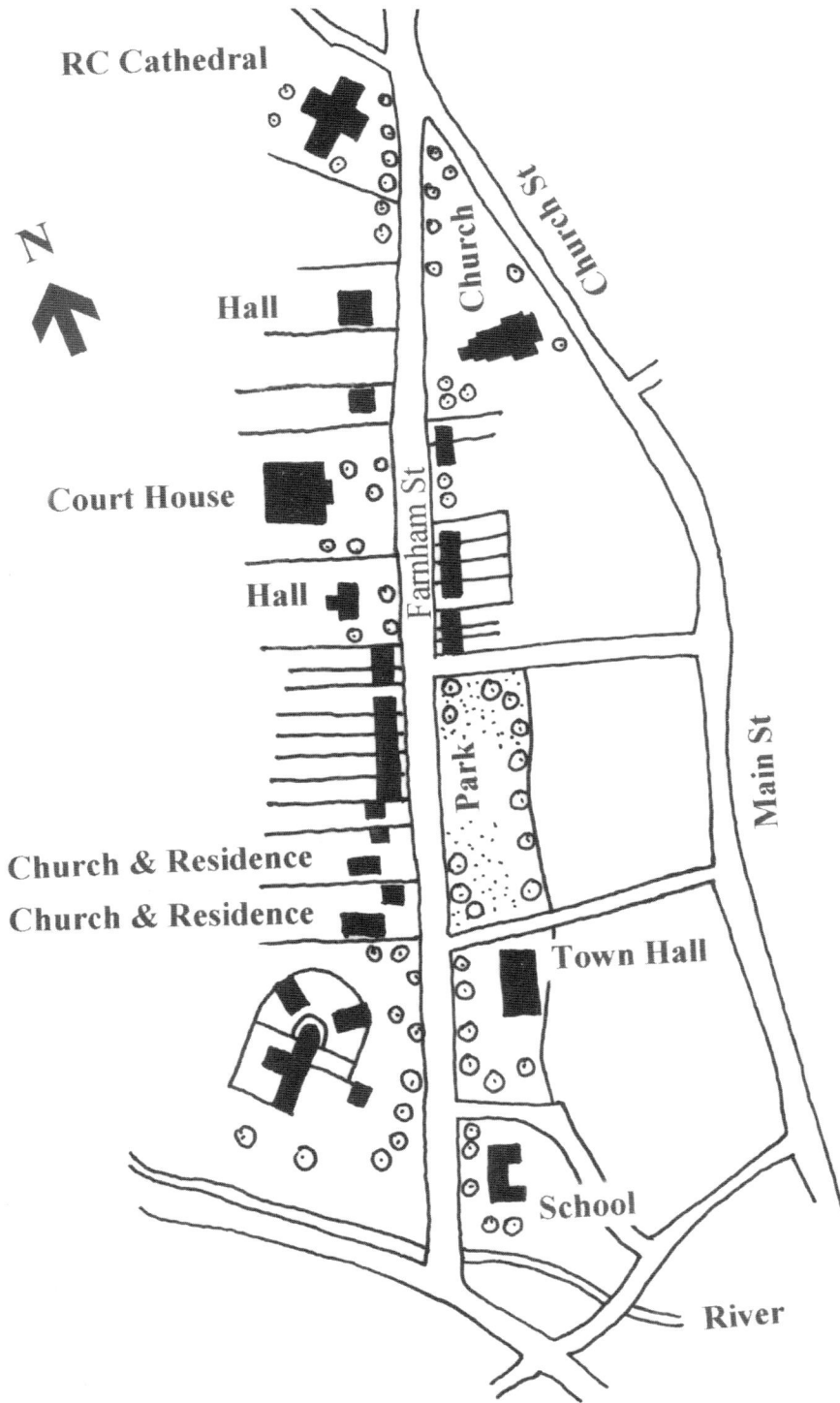

Fig.108: Plan of Farnham Street, Cavan, County Cavan.

traveller. The growth of Tramore, Bangor, Bray, Greystones, Kilkee, and Portrush, for example, can be seen as a response to the growth of holiday travel to the seaside. In this context, Bray and Greystones experienced particularly dramatic expansion, as, in addition to their sea-side facilities, they had the added advantage of being able to act as suburban outliers for the expanding Dublin.

The town of Bray in north County Wicklow had its origins in the medieval period, and until the middle of the nineteenth century consisted of a single street, Main Street, which curved gently southwards, from a bridge across the River Dargle. By the mid-nineteenth century, Bray had already acquired a reputation as a notable sea-side holiday destination, despite the fact that the town was separated from the coastline by a wide stretch of undeveloped land. In 1854, Bray's potential as a holiday resort was considerably boosted when William Dargan introduced the railway to the town; in addition to which, he became involved in the large-scale development which followed. This consisted of four major elements which stretched along the coast parallel to the old town: a new harbour at the estuary of the Dargle, a railway station, an extensive grid of residential streets, and a continuous landscaped esplanade along the sea front (Fig. 109).

The railway line was laid out parallel to, but a short distance inland from, the coastline. A new bridge carried the railway line over the River Dargle, near its mouth, and a new harbour was laid out. South of the bridge, the railway line was laid out on a raised embankment. The railway line effectively acted as a spine, with development taking place on both sides. On the coastal side, Strand Road was laid out parallel to the railway and the landscaped esplanade was built along the seafront. On the landward side, a grid of new Victorian streets linked the new network to the old town. Access to the beach and esplanade was by means of stone archways which were built under the railway embankment.

Fig. 109: Esplanade, Bray, County Wicklow.

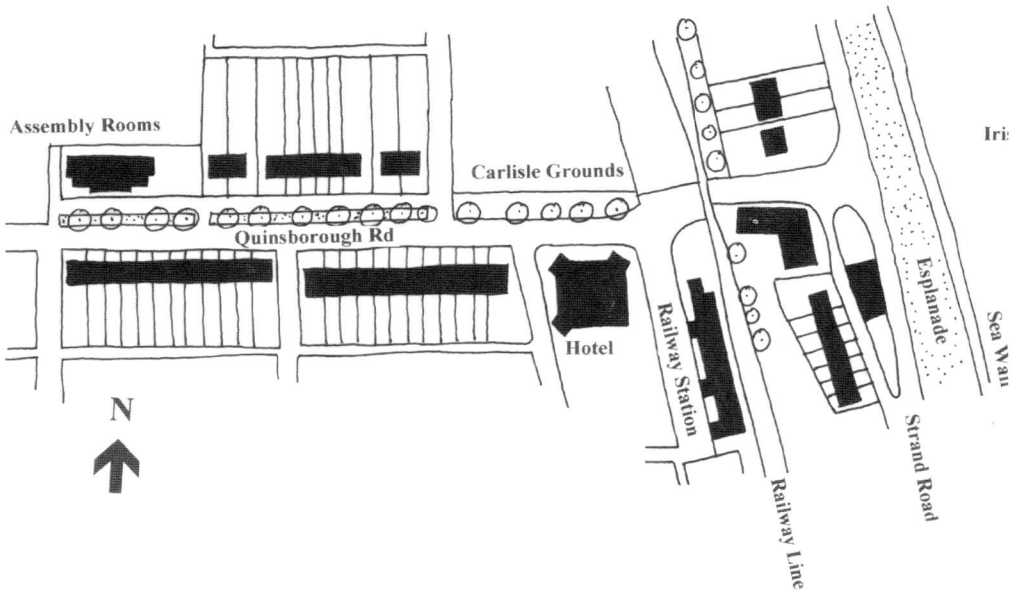

Fig. 110: Layout of Victorian Bray, County Wicklow.

The most significant road in the network was the Quinsborough Road axis, which stretched from the northern end of the older Main Street as far as the seafront (Fig. 110). At its western end, the road was laid out in a characteristic eighteenth-century fashion, with a narrow carriageway flanked on both sides by terraced housing, with doorways opening directly off the footpath. This format was changed about one third of the way along the route, when a more landscaped approach was adopted. At the same time, the blocks were stepped back from the street edge, so as to provide front gardens to the houses, and a tree-lined margin and a service road were included on the north side of the road. In addition, the elevations of the terraces changed from red brick to painted rendering (Fig. 111).

At the eastern end of the street, the axis was continued across the railway line and terminated at the seafront Esplanade. In addition to the standard residential terraces, a number of public buildings and landscape features were incorporated into street. These included the Assembly Rooms, two hotels, and the Carlisle sports grounds. For the most part, the new streets of Bray were lined with typically ornate Victorian houses. These were laid out mainly in terraced fashion and included a range of imposing hotel, public and administrative buildings.

On the opposite side of the country, Kilkee consisted of a small town on the edge of a sandy horseshoe-shaped bay on the western seaboard of County Clare. Like Bray, Kilkee had, by the early nineteenth century, acquired a reputation as a seaside resort and attracted many visitors, particularly from Limerick. These visitors travelled down the Shannon by riverboat, landed at Kilrush, and then travelled the last ten kilometres overland to Kilkee. In 1861, the landlord, the Marquis of Cunningham, recognised the tourism potential of his town and he launched a major regeneration programme which included the demolition of older sections of the town and the laying out of a new plan.

Fig. 111: Quinsborough Road, Bray, County Wicklow.

The new arrangement consisted of a half-circle grid plan. The base of the half-circle was formed by the line of the new esplanade, which was laid along the seafront, while the arc of the circular roads acted as the eastern boundary. Inside this, a network of streets and open spaces was laid out. This included O'Connell Street, the main perpendicular axis of the grid, and the small central market place (Fig. 112).

In 1892, Kilkee's potential as a holiday destination was vastly improved when the West Clare Railway line was extended to the town and a rail terminal was established just outside the line of the southern Circular Road. As with most Victorian towns, the fabric of Kilkee was made up of residential and administrative buildings. The residential architecture consisted, for the most part, of modest single- and double-storey housing which was laid out in terraces. By 1900, the town had expanded to such an extent that it could boast four churches, a convent, two schools, the rail terminus, sea baths, a coast guard station, a court house and a constabulary barracks – all randomly distributed around the town. The layout has one unusual feature, in that landscape within the town was limited to small front gardens. Perhaps the Marquis felt that the extensive beach, the rocky foreshores, and the open sea offered sufficient landscape for their needs of both the residents and the visitors.

ARTISAN DEVELOPMENTS

As was the case in Dublin, most of the regional Victorian centres incorporated artisan housing projects of one sort or another. In the smaller examples, these developments consisted of just a few cottages inserted into the otherwise standard Victorian street arrangement. In the larger centres, such as Cork and Galway, high density projects like the examples in Dromcondra and Irishtown in Dublin were a common feature. One example, which was typical of those found in the larger centres, was Dickson's Lane in Limerick, now demolished (Fig. 113). This consisted of a large number of small single-storey cottages, which were crammed into a restricted triangular site, located near the city's railway station. The layout consisted of an irregular grid of tiny lanes, into which were inserted over 150 cottages, most with only a token enclosed backyard.

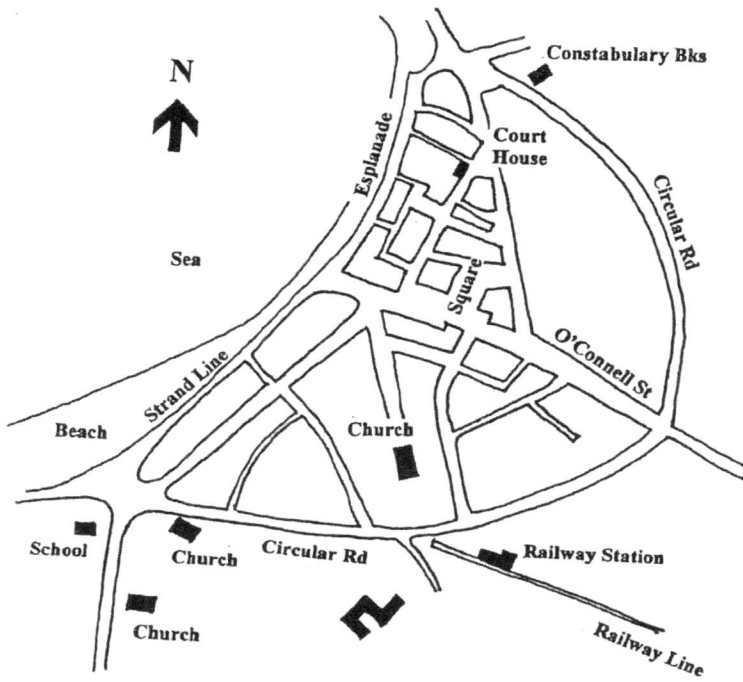

Fig.112: Layout, Kilkee, County Clare.

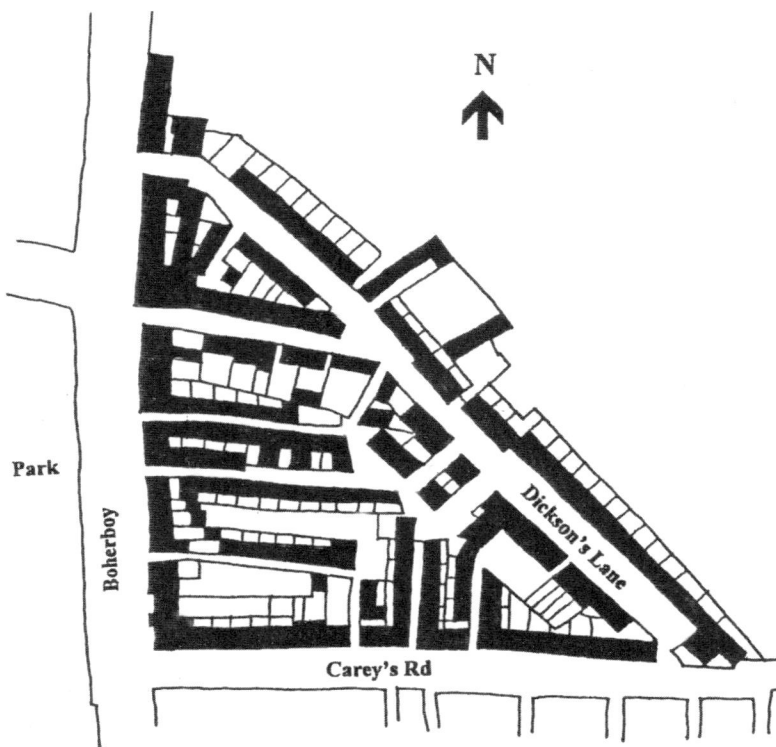

Fig.113: Plan of Dixon's Lane, Limerick, County Limerick.

GREYSTONES

The town of Greystones in County Wicklow is one of the few new Victorian towns to have been laid out on a green field position. In 1838, the coastal site of Greystones consisted of a few scattered fishermen's cottages. By 1900, however, a fully developed town, with all its services, had been established, with an extensive infrastructure that included a harbour, three churches, a convent, three hotels, a parade of shops, a village hall, a coastguard station, a lifeboat station, a post office, a bank, a constabulary barracks, a public park, and a railway station (Fig.114).

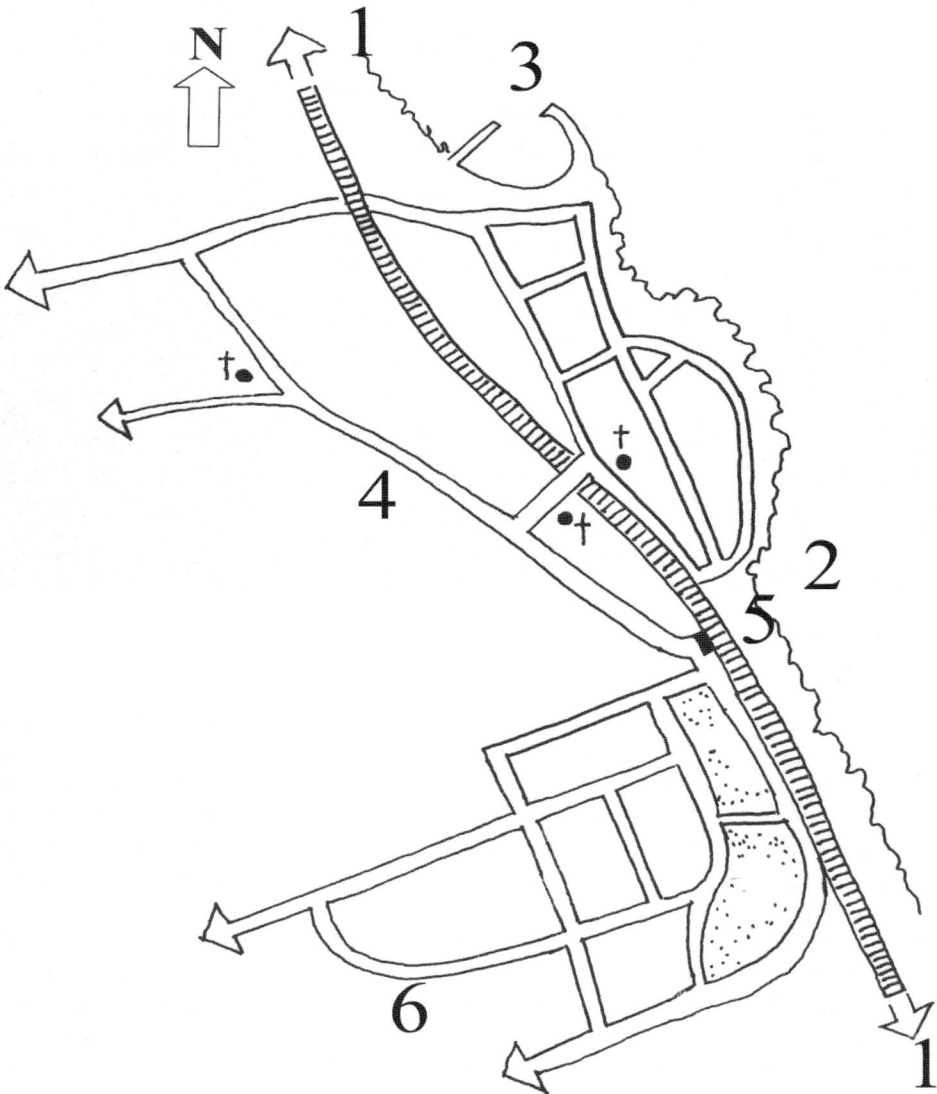

Fig.114: Layout of Greystones, County Wicklow, 1900. (1: Railway Line. 2: Coastline. 3: Harbour. 4: Church Road. 5: Railway Station. 6: Burnaby Estate.)

Fig.115: Terraced Housing, Greystones, County Wicklow.

The development of the town was undertaken by the La Touche and the Burnaby families, although no formal town plan seems to have existed. Instead, the town just grew in a sequence of unconnected stages. The railway arrived in 1856, and the line acted as the spine of the town, with the fabric distributed along both sides. On the sea side, the two principal streets ran parallel to the rail rack, while a third street followed the curved line of the rocky coast. This street pattern was linked to the inshore western side of the town by a stone-built underpass on the northern end and a bridge near the southern end.

Inland of the railway line, the linear Church Street was laid out roughly parallel to the railway line and acted as the major axis of the town. The Church of St Patrick was positioned near the northern end of the axis, while the railway station acted as the termination of the southern end. The La Touche family were the major developers of this northern sector of the town.

Immediately south of the Railway Station, the Burnaby Estate was responsible for laying out a large housing development on a grid layout. The houses in the Burnaby were for the greater part substantial detached and semi-detached houses, built mainly in an imitation Tudor style, while elsewhere in the town the housing consisted of a range of large individual houses, terraced houses (Fig.115) as well as terraced and ornate cottages, mostly set in landscaped gardens.

Victorian town development in Ireland, modest as it was, continued into the early twentieth century, until the combined forces of the First World War, the Easter Rebellion, the War of Independence, the Civil War and the Economic War, brought about a pause. This only began to ease around the middle of the twentieth century, when new forms of legislation, planning ideas, architecture, and ownership came into play. This new twentieth-century town development phase was, however, so extensive in scale, scope and variety of building types that it lies outside the scope of this guide. In fact so different, so complex and so far reaching are its impacts that it warrants a guide of its own.

NINE

GAZETTEER

IRISH TOWNS

This gazetteer offers a list of selected centres that are representative of Ireland's historic towns. The list is set out on a county-by-county basis, and highlights the significant historical phases that are on offer in each of the individual towns. Those centres mentioned in the main text are marked with an asterisk where appropriate.

ULSTER

COUNTY ANTRIM

Carrickfergus: Norman foundation expanded during the Plantation period. Surviving elements include: Norman wedge-shaped street and a magnificent castle. Also part of Plantation town defences.

Belfast: Exceptional Victorian development of grid planning and street architecture. Vast grid street layout with good public building and extensive Victorian housing.

COUNTY ARMAGH

Armagh: Early Christian curved street plan. Excellent Georgian sector with landscaped mall, public buildings, and housing.

Lurgan: Plantation town, with a central diamond and long axial street.

COUNTY CAVAN

Cavan: Excellent Victorian sector with public buildings and housing.
Ballyjamesduff: Irregular Georgian grid.

COUNTY DONEGAL

Donegal: Plantation town with diamond and castle.

Ballyshannon: Plantation town with diamond.

Letterkenny: Plantation town.

COUNTY DOWN

★*Castlewellan*: Excellent example of Georgian planning with double market place.

Newtownards: Plantation foundation with good Georgian grid layout and square.

★*Newry*: Plantation foundation, with excellent Georgian layout and squares.

Warrenpoint: Excellent grid town with harbour and squares.

COUNTY FERMANAGH

Enniskillen: Plantation town, laid out on irregular grid with a market square.

COUNTY DERRY

★*Coleraine*: Excellent example of Plantation grid layout.

★*Derry*: Exceptional example of Plantation grid street plan and town wall.

COUNTY MONAGHAN

★*Monaghan*: Plantation town with market square and extending streets.

Clones: Early Christian settlement with Plantation diamond. Surviving Early Christian elements include a round tower, high cross, and church.

Castleblaney: Plantation town with diamond.

LEINSTER

COUNTY CARLOW

Bagnalstown: Interesting Georgian gridiron town plan.

Tullow: Small town with central market square.

COUNTY DUBLIN

Dublin: Exceptional multi-sector city with Viking street plan, as well as impressive Norman, Georgian, and Victorian sectors. Surviving elements include the medieval fabric, and parts of town wall; Georgian streets, squares, and fabric; and Victorian streets, squares, and fabric.

COUNTY KILDARE

Kildare: Excellent example of Early Christian settlement. Surviving elements include: curved-street layout, triangular market place, round tower.

Monasterevin: Small Georgian town. Surviving elements include a linear grid, market square, and Grand Canal harbour.

COUNTY KILKENNY

Kilkenny: Excellent example of multi-sector town. Early Christian foundation and Norman town. Surviving elements include an Early Christian curved-street pattern and round tower. Also Norman linear streets, a magnificent castle, a cathedral, a ruined Franciscan friary, an Augustinian priory, a restored Dominican friary, seventeenth-century houses, stretches of town wall and gate, and a wall tower.

Castlecomer: Interesting town with Early Christian, Norman, Georgian, and Victorian elements.

COUNTY LAOIS

Portarlington: Plantation town laid out around central market square.

Port Laoise: Plantation town laid out around fort.

COUNTY LONGFORD

Edgeworthstown: Small Georgian town with axial street.

Granard: Georgian linear town, with Norman motte-and-bailey at one end.

Longford: Georgian town with irregular grid plan and small central triangular green.

COUNTY LOUTH

Ardee: Norman linear town. Surviving elements include a pair of tower houses, a church, and a medieval college.

Drogheda: Excellent Norman grid town. Surviving elements include: parts of town wall, gate, motte-and-bailey, ruins of Dominican friary and Augustinian priory.

Carlingford: Exceptional example of Norman grid town. Surviving elements include a castle, tower houses, market place, town wall, and ruins of Dominican priory.

COUNTY MEATH

Kells: Outstanding Early Christian foundation. Surviving elements include a curved street plan, round tower, church, and high crosses. Also part of medieval town wall.

Trim: Norman town laid out on both sides of River Boyne. Surviving elements include the market place, magnificent castle, part of town wall, and gate.

COUNTY OFFALLY

Birr: Dual-sector town with Norman street, market place, and castle. Outstanding Georgian sector. Surviving elements include an axial street, two market squares, two malls, and excellent fabric.

Tullamore: Regular grid of Georgian streets, two market squares, and a canal harbour.

COUNTY WESTMEATH

Athlone: Two Norman sectors linked across the River Shannon by a bridge. Both sectors laid out on an irregular street pattern. Impressive riverside castle and stretch of town wall.

Kilbeggan: Small planned Georgian town, arranged around a central market square, with canal harbour.

Mullingar: Norman linear town. Town fabric mainly Victorian as is the dramatic sweep of Royal Canal which flows around the north side of the town.

COUNTY WEXFORD

Wexford: Interesting multi-sector town. Partial remains of Early Christian foundation. Little remains of Viking sector. Extensive Norman grid sector. Surviving Norman elements include: curved central axis, part of town wall.

Gorey: Plantation foundation with gridiron street layout.

New Ross: Large Norman irregular grid town. Surviving elements include sections of town wall, tower, and remains of a parish church.

COUNTY WICKLOW

Bray: Multi-sector town. Norman foundation. Georgian Main street. Good Victorian sector with seafront. Nothing survives of medieval Bray. Surviving elements include line of Georgian Main Street; Victorian esplanade, harbour, line of railway, square, and range of Victorian architecture.

Greystones: New Victorian town with irregular street layout. Surviving elements include a harbour, line of railway, sea road, and interesting range of street architecture.

MUNSTER

COUNTY CLARE

Ennis: Norman town with irregular street pattern and some fabric.

Kilkee: Interesting Victorian seaside town. Surviving elements include a semi-circular plan, an axial street, extensive seafront promenade and interesting fabric.

COUNTY CORK

Cork: Interesting multi-sector city. Early Christian settlement. Site of Viking town uncertain. Cross-linear Norman town. Surprisingly few surviving medieval elements. Very unusual and sinuous Georgian street plan, formed by the covering over of the side channels of the River Lee.

Youghal: Excellent Norman linear town with basetown suburb. Surviving elements include part of town wall, a tower house, and a ruined Dominican friary.

Fermoy: Interesting Georgian town with axial plan and square.

Mitchelstown: Excellent example of Georgian grid town with squares and axial streets.

Kinsale: Highly complex Norman town with basetown suburb. Surviving elements include: part of town wall and a parish church.

COUNTY KERRY

Tralee: Norman foundation with no remains. Irregular Georgian street grid with market square.

Listowel: Norman foundation with surviving castle. Georgian sector with market square.

Kenmare: Georgian foundation with an unusual X-shaped plan.

COUNTY LIMERICK

★*Limerick*: Outstanding multi-sector city. Excellent Norman town with castle, cathedral, stretches of town wall, town gate, and the ruins of two tower houses. Outstanding example of Georgian gridiron street layout with squares, crescent, axial streets, excellent public buildings, and housing. Extensive Victorian sectors with religious buildings, military barracks, market, jail, hospital, mental hospital, cemetery, and housing.

★*Kilmallock*: Outstanding cross-linear Norman layout. Surviving elements include: tower house, friary, extensive town wall, and town gate.

COUNTY TIPPERARY

Roscrea: Interesting multi-sector town. Early Christian site. Surviving elements include: round tower, part of church. Norman sectors with castle. Irregular Georgian sector with market square and mall.

★*Fethard*: Outstanding example of Norman town. Surviving elements include: wedged-shaped street, parish church, tower houses, market house, almost entire town wall, wall towers, and gate.

Cahir: Norman foundation with outstanding castle. Also Georgian sector with market square.

COUNTY WATERFORD

★*Waterford*: Extensive Viking street plan. Also extensive Norman street plan. Surviving elements include: tower, abbey ruins, parts of town wall, wall towers.

Dungarvan: Dual sector town. Norman sector laid out on grid, with ruins of riverside castle. Also interesting Georgian sector with axial layout and central square.

CONNACHT

COUNTY GALWAY

★*Athenry*: Outstanding example of an irregular Norman grid. Surviving elements include a market square, extensive town wall, gatehouse, exceptional castle, and ruined Dominican friary.

Galway: Excellent Norman grid street plan. Surviving elements include a market place, parish church, water gate, and parts of the town wall.

Loughrea: Interesting Norman grid. Surviving elements include a market place, tower house, and the ruins of Carmelite friary. The still-active moat is a unique feature.

COUNTY LEITRIM

★Jamestown: Small and interesting Plantation town. Parts of town wall and gate survive.

Carrick-on-Shannon: Plantation town.

COUNTY MAYO

★*Westport*: Exceptional Georgian town with axial street plan, octagon, and mall.

Castlebar: Georgian layout with square and mall.

COUNTY ROSCOMMON

Roscommon: Norman foundation. Planned Plantation sector seems never to have been built. Now a Georgian axial town with market square.

COUNTY SLIGO

Sligo: Norman town laid out on a grid. Surviving remains include a ruined medieval friary with chapter house. Also site of seventeenth-century fort.